D1917097

Interest

CONCEPTS IN THE SOCIAL SCIENCES
Series editor: Frank Parkin

Published titles

Democracy (Second Edition)	*Anthony Arblaster*
Discrimination	*Michael Banton*
Citizenship	*J. M. Barbalet*
Welfare (Second Edition)	*Norman Barry*
Freedom	*Zygmunt Bauman*
Bureaucracy (Second Edition)	*David Beetham*
Nationalism	*Craig Calhoun*
Trotskyism	*Alex Callinicos*
Revolution and Counter-Revolution	*Peter Calvert*
Policy (Second Edition)	*H. K. Colebatch*
Socialism	*Bernard Crick*
Exchange	*John Davis*
Social Science	*Gerard Delanty*
Social Darwinism	*Peter Dickens*
Power	*Keith Dowding*
Rights	*Michael Freeden*
Feminism	*Jane Freedman*
Science	*Steve Fuller*
Liberalism (Second Edition)	*John Gray*
The State	*John A. Hall and G. John Ikenberry*
Kinship	*C. C. Harris*
Sovereignty	*John Hoffman*
Discourse	*David Howarth*
Utopianism	*Krishan Kumar*
Social Structure	*Jose Lopez and John Scott*
Postmodernity (Second Edition)	*David Lyon*
Ideology (Second Edition)	*David McLellan*
Pluralism	*Gregor McLennan*
Fascism	*Mark Neocleous*
Conservatism	*Robert Nisbet*
Structuration	*John Parker*
Race and Ethnicity	*John Rex*
Postcommunism	*Richard Sakwa*
Orientalism	*Ziauddin Sardar*
Capitalism	*Peter Saunders*
Class	*Richard Scase*
Caste	*Ursula Sharma*
Ecologism	*Mark J. Smith*
Culture	*Mark J. Smith*
Polulism	*Paul Taggart*
Status	*Bryan S. Turner*
Multiculturalism	*C. W. Watson*
Risk	*Roy Boyne*
Interest	*Richard Swedberg*

Interest

Richard Swedberg

Open University Press

Open University Press
McGraw-Hill Education
McGraw-Hill House
Shoppenhangers Road
Maidenhead
Berkshire
England
SL6 2QL

email: enquiries@openup.co.uk
world wide web: www.openup.co.uk

and Two Penn Plaza, New York, NY 10121-2289, USA

First published 2005

A catalogue record of this book is available from the British Library

ISBN-13 978 0335 21614 7 (pb) 978 0335 21615 4 (pb)
ISBN-10 0335 21614 5 (pb) 0335 21615 3 (hb)

Library of Congress Cataloging-in-Publication Data
CIP data applied for

Typeset by YHT Ltd
Printed in the UK by Bell & Bain Ltd, Glasgow

Contents

Preface

> Concepts lead us to make investigations;
> are the expression of our interest,
> and direct our interest.
> Wittgenstein, *Philosophical Investigations*

There are many concepts that are part of the vocabulary of the social sciences but have not yet had the discussion that they deserve. The concept of interest is one of these, and in the pages to come I will attempt to outline the ways in which it has been used, and various attempts to define it. My own discipline is that of sociology but I have tried to cover the use of the concept of interest in other disciplines as well, especially economics and political science.

The material that a thorough discussion of the concept of interest should cover is enormous, and my attempts at intellectual triage have, I hope, been the right ones. I have also made a concerted effort to give a voice to many of the individual authors who have drawn on the concept of interest at the same time as I have criticized them; and a good balance between these two tasks has not always been easy to strike.

The main theme in Chapter 1 is interest and its many traditions. When we look at the way that the concept of interest has been used throughout the centuries, I argue, we find a richness of different uses, and many of these may serve as an inspiration today. Chapter 2 is devoted to the topic of how the concept of interest slowly became transformed into a social science concept during the nineteenth century; and the key issue here is what was gained and lost in the process. Chapter 3 tells the story of the way that sociologists have tried to incorporate the concept of interest into their theories, from the classics up to today; and, again, an attempt has been made to sort the wheat from the chaff. In Chapter 4 I discuss the way that the concept of interest has been used in modern political science and economics. I also present a new approach to the concept of interest: what it means and how it should be used. I have tried to address the question of interest from a radically different perspective, and the reader will be the judge of its worth.

The book ends with an addendum devoted to an issue that has not been discussed in the existing literature, namely interest as a policy concept. Because of the absence of material on this topic, I have chosen to address it in the form of a case study. The case I have chosen is conflict-of-interest legislation and its role in the corporate scandals that have recently occurred in the United States.

I am grateful to Frank Parkin, who is the editor of this series, for giving me some very helpful criticism. I also wish to thank Philippe Schmitter for kindly allowing me to use some unpublished material on the concept of interest which he produced in the early 1980s. For advice, inspiration and information about the concept of interest and its many uses, I finally also want to thank my friends and colleagues Patrik Aspers, Pierre Demeulenaere, Johan Heilbron, Victor Nee and Geir Øygarden.

The book is dedicated to Mabel Berezin.

R.S.

1

Interest and its Many Traditions

A classical question in social science is 'What causes people to act the way that they do?' An equally classical answer is 'their interests'. Given the importance of the concept of interest, one would assume that it has been discussed quite a bit and also that there exists some clarity about its meaning and how it should be used. This, however, is not the case; and this study is, as of today, the fullest that exists in English. The reason for this neglect is not easy to understand, but is perhaps related to the fact that the concept of interest played a fundamental role in analysing people's behaviour long before modern social science came into being, and is therefore part of what is being taken for granted.

The concept of interest is often and easily used in a number of different contexts, from everyday language to political and social science discourses. Its meaning may seem self-evident and in little need of definition beyond the statement that interest is an important force that drives or determines the behaviour of people and of groups. We all know that people can be self-interested; that a country may have interests in other parts of the world; and that there are plenty of interest groups in political life. This flexibility of the concept of interest – that it can so easily be used in many different contexts and to analyse many different phenomena – is, I will argue, one of its many positive qualities.

There are, no doubt, some drawbacks to this flexibility as well – for example, that it makes the concept of interest difficult to nail down – but for the moment I want to continue on the theme of flexibility and its positive implications. First of all, there is the important fact that the concept of interest has been used, and is being used, in so many of the social sciences. It is a key concept in economics, sociology, political science and history. One can also find it in philosophy, law, pedagogy and a few other disciplines as well. People who are active in practical life – in law, politics and so on – also use the concept of interest. What all of this adds up to is that those who want to use the concept of interest are in a position to draw on a number of different traditions and, within each of these, on a number of different uses. The result is a richness that is rare for a social science concept; and one of the goals that I want to accomplish with this study is to draw attention to many of the ingenious ways in which the concept of interest has been used by sociologists, economists, political scientists, politicians and so on.

The richness of ideas that can be found in the many traditions that have drawn on the concept of interest is, however, not very much appreciated today; and the main reason for this is as follows. The concept of interest, and even more so the concept of self-interest, has in recent discourse had its meaning drastically reduced to a single one, namely that of *economic self-interest*. To the economists – and it is the economists who have set the tone in this respect – interest is identical to self-interest, and it is also something that can be measured according to a universal metric, usually money. It matters little if the actors are inspired by, say, altruism or if they are unsure whether they can realize their interests; altruism can be cast in terms of self-interest, and uncertainty in terms of probability and risk.

The economists' way of looking at interest has obvious advantages when it comes to formalizing the analysis, which is often stressed by those who are its advocates. But it also stands in sharp contrast to the rich and complex ways in which the notion of interest has been used over the centuries by people such as La Rochefoucauld, David Hume, Adam Smith, Alexis de Tocqueville, Karl Marx, Max Weber and many others. To them, interest was a very handy and flexible concept that could be molded to some specific task at hand and that, as a consequence, appeared in many different shapes. It should also be noted that during its first few centuries of existence, the concept of interest was not so much used as a central principle which might serve as the foundation for a whole system of thought, as in modern economics, but rather to make sense of single situations that defied an easy understanding, say, the relationship between sin and virtue (Mandeville), self-interest and general interest (Adam Smith), and the like.

For these and other reasons it is incorrect, as I see it, to speak of the concept of interest as if it has one and only one meaning that can somehow be distilled from all of its uses and then presented to the reader in the form of a clever definition. The concept of interest is rather to be understood as an uncommonly rich and broad concept that can be taken in different directions, as shown by the many uses to which it has been put by La Rochefoucauld, David Hume, Adam Smith and so on. Albert O. Hirschman writes in *The Passions and the Interests* that from the 1600s onwards one may speak of interest as 'a new paradigm' in which many types of problems and analyses found their place (Hirschman 1977: 42). I agree with Hirschman that the emergence of the concept of interest in the West indeed signals the birth of a new perspective. It is also a concept that has come to have more meanings than most social science concepts and which therefore lends itself to being used in theories that otherwise do not go very well together. Marx, for example, uses the concept of interest and so does Weber – who disagrees with Marx on many points, and so on.

It may well be possible to both speak about interest as a new paradigm or a new perspective as well as about its many uses in different theories. This chapter is primarily devoted to an exploration of the multitude of uses that the concept of interest has had over the centuries, but I will also try to nail down its general meaning to the extent that this can be done.

Before making a brief historical account of the evolution of the concept of interest, from the late Middle Ages till today, it may be helpful to introduce some conceptual distinctions. One of these has to do with the explanatory power that has been assigned to the concept of interest in the various theories. There is also the fact that some analysts have used a unitary and single type of interest, while others have drawn on a number of different kinds of interest, such as economic interests, political interests, sexual interests and so on. Interests are often seen as having a time dimension; they can be short term or long term, for example. It is also assumed that actors are sometimes aware of their interests and at other times they are not. And, finally, interests can be seen as given or as constructed.

These distinctions are all central and a few lines of explication will therefore be devoted to each of them. How much explanatory power interests are to have in the analysis, for example, can be said to range from everything to nothing. In the former case, the concept of interest threatens to become a tautology. Many thinkers in the seventeenth century, for example, use interest to explain practically everything – as do some economists today. For an early illustration of the tendency to turn interest into *the* explanation of the social world, one can cite the well-known statement by Helvétius: 'As the physical world is ruled by the laws of movement, so is the moral universe ruled by the laws of interest' (Helvétius [1758] 2000: 42).

In several types of modern sociology, in contrast, interests are either seen as having no or very little influence on what is happening. According to so-called relational sociology, for example, it is old-fashioned and wrong to explain things through 'substances' (such as interests); everything should be seen in terms of relations, and only relations can be used to explain (e.g. Emirbayer 1997). There is also new institutionalism in organizational sociology, which does see some role for interests in the explanation – but a very small one indeed and also one that it tends to ignore (e.g. DiMaggio 1988). Finally, it is quite common in contemporary sociology to mention the importance of social relations, social structures and norms – but to leave out interests.

Most analyses in which interest is central typically situate themselves somewhere between the position that leads to a tautology and the one that assumes that interest has little or no impact. Exactly where to draw the line is naturally a contested issue as well as an extremely important one. Many battles in Marxism have, for example, been fought out over exactly what role should be assigned to economic interests versus political interests and ideology. As this example also shows, the answer may vary with the type of interest that is involved.

This last remark leads in a natural way to another distinction that needs to be made, and it has to do with the issue of whether one should work with a single and unitary type of interest or with many different types of interest. Usually, when it is a question of assigning central importance to a single and unitary kind of interest, it is economic interest that is being discussed. Mainstream economics, for example, has equated interest exclusively with economic interest since around 1900; and, as already mentioned, there exists today a general tendency in social science to do the same and to ignore the rich tradition of interest analysis that has developed over the centuries. In this latter tradition, in contrast, it is very common to operate with a number of different interests, such as ideal interests, material interests, political interest and so on. The assumption of a multiplicity of interests can of course raise the issue of tautology as well, even if it is in a somewhat different form than the one mentioned earlier. It also raises many difficult questions about the priority among the different kinds of interests; whether it is possible to arrange these in some kind of order, and so on. No general answers have been given to these types of questions, and probably cannot be given. None the less, it is also clear (as will soon be shown) that the assumption of a multiplicity of interests adds considerably to the flexibility of the analysis and invites a different type of skill from the side of the analyst.

A related distinction is that of time; while some interests are seen as short term, others are seen as long term. In modern economic analysis this distinction is sometimes handled through the idea of discounting, that is, one takes some metric and then proceeds on the assumption that unit X will decrease with an identical amount during each time period. But there also exist other ways of dealing with this issue as, for example, Tocqueville shows in *Democracy in America* and which may better reflect the origin of this distinction, which is religious in nature. Long-term interests, in brief, were those that referred to life after death in Christianity, while short-term interest referred to life on earth (Holmes 1990: 343). Tocqueville's argument in *Democracy in America* is that religion allows the Americans to realize their real or long-term interests by choosing *not* to give in to short-term or distracting interests (Tocqueville [1835–40] 2000: 600–6). In this particular example – and this is why it was chosen – one cannot use the idea of discounting, since we are not talking of items or activities that can be reduced to a common unit.

A further distinction that can be found among the many ways of handling interest in social science analysis has to do with the actors' level of awareness of the interests involved. This is where concepts such as false consciousness, ideology, self-deception and so on come into the picture; and these are not easy to handle. One way of cutting through a few of the difficulties is to distinguish between analyses that are empirical in nature and those that are normative. An empirical analysis in this context would be one in which the level of awareness is investigated empirically. Do the actors speak of their interests (or some equivalent term), and how aware are they of, say, (1) which these interests are, (2) how they can be reached, and (3) what consequences their realization will have? The normative approach differs in that it operates on the assumption that full awareness is desirable and that lack of such awareness should be overcome. A normative approach can, for example, be found in

Marx, where it is mainly a question of becoming aware of one's class interests, and in Freud, where the transparency of one's sexual interests is at issue.

The final distinction I want to take up is the one between the assumption of interests as given and interests as socially constructed. Having just referred to Freud, it is clear that biological interests belong to the category of given interests. But so do interests in mainstream economic analysis to some extent, and the reason for this is that this type of analysis operates on the assumption that preferences are given. Similarly, socially constructed interests cover, on the one hand, the situation where certain interests are collectively created and therefore appear as given to the individual. On the other hand, there are also situations where individuals may construct their own interests, more or less as they see fit. An individual may, for example, choose to join a certain religious group but usually cannot create a religion.

The History of the Concept of Interest, or Its Many Rich Traditions

There exist a very small number of writings that attempt to cover the history of the concept of interest, typically in the form of brief articles or entries in encyclopedias or dictionaries. One's first reaction when reading some of these is often confusion, since they present a large number of uses and definitions in quick succession, typically without any attempt to tie them together. In a few pages the reader is confronted with a collage of political, economic and philosophical approaches to interest. The whole thing is also experienced as dissatisfying for the following two reasons: no straightforward and usable definition of interest is given, and the account typically comes in the form of a rather old-fashioned type of history of ideas.

It is definitely correct that the existing literature on the concept of interest does not contain one single and useful definition of interest, which can easily be operationalized. While all social science concepts have a certain tendency to be a bit like clouds that look solid from a distance but evaporate once you come closer, it also would appear that this tendency is particularly strong when it comes to the concept of interest.

There are several reasons for this, as I see it, including the fact that the concept of interest has been used during many centuries, in many different contexts and in many different disciplines. And this brings us back to what was said in connection with the discussion of interest as a paradigm (Hirschman), namely that this concept has a certain umbrella-like quality to it and covers a number of different theories and approaches. While this in no way lessens the need for a solid definition, in this particular chapter I will instead point to its positive side, namely that the concept of interest has had multiple uses, many of which are still instructive. Before rushing to seek unity, in short, it may be useful to explore this richness; and it is in this spirit that I suggest that we approach the history of the concept of interest.

The second objection to the standard histories of the concept is that they have been written from the perspective of a rather old-fashioned form of history of ideas. This means that they basically restrict themselves to a presentation of what various key figures in Western thought have said on the topic, one after the other, without much of a link between these different opinions, except for some particular point that the author wants to make.

What is currently missing from this type of literature, in brief, is an approach that would be more social in nature – something along the lines of sociological or historical semantics or even what Foucault has called the history of thought with its emphasis on the context in which people start using some term or concept (e.g. Foucault 2001). While everyday usages of the concept of interest may be impossible to establish today, especially when it is a question of a time long past, this would still be one of the goals of this type of work. Particular attention from this perspective would also be devoted to different groups of intellectuals, and how the concept of interest has travelled from one to the other, typically losing as well as adding meanings during its voyage.

While studies of this type will, I hope, be produced in the future, in the meantime one has to use what exists. The best accounts of the history of the concept of interest that have been produced up till now are Albert O. Hirschman's 'The Concept of Interest: From Euphemism to Tautology' and Stephen Holmes' 'The Secret History of Self-Interest' (Hirschman 1986, Holmes 1990). If one also includes literature in other languages than English, a special mention should be made of the articles on interest in the German encyclopaedia *Geschichtliche Grundbegriffe* (Orth *et al.* 1982; see also e.g. Huber 1958, Neuendorff 1973). Some fine studies of single episodes in the history of the concept of interest also exist, such as

The Passions and the Interests by Albert O. Hirschman and *Politics and the Public Interest in the Seventeenth Century* by J.A.W. Gunn (Hirschman 1977, Gunn 1969; see also e.g. Heilbron 1998).

In the rest of this chapter I will first present a brief history of the concept of interest, based on the literature just mentioned, and then discuss the view of interest that one can find among a few select authors such as La Rochefoucauld, Adam Smith and David Hume. The general reason for proceeding in this manner is to give the reader a sense of the richness of the different traditions of the concept of interest and, more generally, of the creative ways in which this concept has been used. I also want to show how one can take single instances when the concept of interest has been used and, through a close scrutiny of these, come up with ideas and hypotheses.

In the entry for 'interest' in the *Oxford English Dictionary* one can read that 'there is much that is obscure in the history of this word [that is, interest]' (OED 1989: 1099). What nearly all students of the history of this term agree on, however, is that 'interest' comes from the Latin *inter-* ('inter-') and *esse* ('to be'); and that it means, among other things, 'to be between' and 'to make a difference'. The only caveat here is that what we are talking about is the *word* interest, as opposed to the *idea* of interest. If we also want to include in our account of the concept of interest the idea of egoism, we would have to start much earlier and include, for example, Greek philosophy (e.g. Rogers 1997).

In the later Middle Ages the concept of interest can be found in Roman legal thought as well as in the economic discourse of the day, in the sense of rate of interest on a loan. There is a direct link between this latter meaning and the original Latin meaning of interest, as is clear from Frank Knight's observation that 'the modern term [of interest on a loan] comes from the Roman law expression for an indemnification for damage due to the delay in the interval (*interesse*) before repayment, one of the chief forms under which payment for loans came to be tolerated by canonical and civil courts' (Knight 1932: 131). It is also sometimes noted that interest in this latter sense can be characterized as a euphemism for usury, and that the concept of interest would be used as a euphemism in several other contexts as well.

One of these other contexts is that of politics; during the seventeenth century the concept of interest became part of political discourse, in writing as well as in everyday language. It was mainly used to describe how a ruler should behave and to analyse his behaviour and understand his real goals. 'Interest will not lie' became a popular political saying in seventeenth-century England; and this statement can both be seen as a prescription for how the ruler should behave (find your interests and follow these) and as a key to the understanding of someone's behaviour (if you understand someone's interest, you will also know how they will behave). The political notion of interest has also been termed a euphemism since it cast the ruthless behaviour of rulers in a language that gives associations to reason and intelligence. While Machiavelli does not use the word 'interest' in *The Prince*, it has been argued that he caught its spirit when he advised the ruler to set aside conventional morality in order to realize his true goals or interests.

A.W. Gunn, who is the main authority on this aspect of the history of the concept of interest, notes that in seventeenth-century England people also had started to speak of different types of interest. Interests could be 'legal', 'landed', 'monied' and so on. Gunn draws on a number of different sources in *Politics and the Public Interest in the Seventeenth Century*, including a large number of political pamphlets; and he also makes an effort to broaden the empirical basis for the historical study of the concept of interest well beyond major works by famous authors.

In *The Passions and the Interests*, which is an excellent work as well as a somewhat old-fashioned study in the tradition of the history of ideas, Albert O. Hirschman argues that the political concept of interest was also used in the seventeenth century in a non-euphemistic and non-cynical manner. The most important example of this that he cites is a work by the Huguenot statesman, the Duke of Rohan, entitled *On the Interest of Princes and States of Christianity* (1638), which became influential in many European countries. The Duke of Rohan's key idea was that interests could be used to counter the passions that drove the rulers to engage in constant warfare and ruin their countries. Interest, as he perceived it, meant primarily a calculating and methodical spirit as opposed to the much more impulsive and destructive nature of the passions.

According to Hirschman, thinkers such as Montesquieu and Sir James Steuart also made the argument that one can apply the concept of interest to *economic affairs* and that these could work as a counterweight to political passions. To trade with one another, they argued, introduces a calm and moderate spirit among the people, according to the famous thesis of *doux commerce*. Or in the words of Sir James Steuart: '[a] modern economy, therefore, is the most effectual bridle ever was invented against the folly of despotism' (Hirschman 1977: 85). Montesquieu says similarly in *The Spirit of the Laws* (1748):

> The spirit of commerce brings with it the spirit of frugality, of economy, of moderation, of work, of wisdom, of tranquility, of order, and of regularity. In this manner, as long as this spirit prevails, the riches it creates do not have any bad effect. (Montesquieu 1989: 71)

The concept of interest also played an important role among the French moralists in the seventeenth century and the members of the Scottish Enlightenment in the eighteenth century. In both of these circles, interest was seen as part of human nature. Many of La Rochefoucauld's famous maxims are, for example, centred around interest. His *Maxims* (1665) opens as follows: 'What we take for virtues are often only a collection of various actions and interests which fortune or our own industry knows how to arrange; and it is not always through valor and chastity that men are valiant and that women are chaste' (La Rochefoucauld 2001: 3).

The two most important figures in the Scottish Enlightenment, from the perspective of the concept of interest, are David Hume and Adam Smith. In the former's *Treatise of Human Nature* (1739–40), interest plays a key role in the discussion of a number of topics, from justice to politics. It is also to Hume that we owe the following well-known statement: 'Nothing is more certain, then that men are, in a great measure, govern'd by interest' (Hume 1978: 534). And no account of Adam Smith fails to mention his discussion of the invisible hand in *The Wealth of Nations* (1776) and how the baker, the brewer and the butcher further the general interest by pursuing their very own private interest.

Just as the concept of interest was extended to the area of politics during the seventeenth century, so it was extended to the area of the economy during the eighteenth and nineteenth centuries. According to Marcel Mauss, the notion of 'individual (economic) interest' is unique to the Western world (Mauss [1925] 1990: 76). As an example of how this development came about, one can mention utilitarianism. In *Table of the Springs of Action* (1817) Jeremy Bentham presented a whole category of different interests, including 'pecuniary interest', and showed how these affect human beings in a positive as well as a negative way. John Stuart Mill similarly drew on a wide variety of interests in his general analysis, even if the first rough draft of *homo economicus* also came from his pen. There is finally also Karl Marx who introduced the notion of class interest.

After the birth of modern (neoclassical) economics around 1900, it is generally agreed that the concept of interest began to lose its flexibility and was reduced to one single interest: *economic interest*. This interest was analysed with the help of a metric and equated with strict self-interest. As the twentieth century progressed, the term 'interest' was first replaced by the more neutral-sounding term 'utility', which in its turn was later replaced by the notion of revealed preferences. Interest, which for some thinkers had primarily been a motive or 'a spring of action', had at this point become what your behaviour revealed and little else. The economic view of things has also, during the last few decades, become quite popular in the other social sciences as well as applied to non-economic topics by the economists; and this has made it ubiquitous. Today, according to Hirschman, the concept of (economic) interest is seen as the explanation of everything, and therefore should be characterized as a tautology.

The Use of the Concept of Interest among the French Moralists (La Rochefoucauld)

That the various traditions of using the concept of interest are rich and suggestive will be illustrated with the help of a few thinkers in this chapter, starting with La Rochefoucauld (1613–80) and his maxims. La Rochefoucauld was part of the French moralists, a group of writers that began with Montaigne but which mainly flourished in the seventeenth century thanks to such people as Pascal and La Bruyère. A main concern of these authors was with morality and its role in different types of human behaviour. The concept of interest played a very important role in these writings, and the French moralists shared their obsession with this concept with other seventeenth- and eighteenth-century French intellectuals. Through a content analysis of several hundred works from the period 1600–1800 in France, it has been shown that there was a sharp increase in the use of the concept of interest from the 1620s onwards, and a corresponding decline from the 1780s onwards (Heilbron 1998: 100–1).

There are two reasons why social scientists, who are concerned with the concept of interest, tend to ignore a writer like La

Rochefoucauld, and these need to be spelled out. The first is related to the fact that his work primarily falls in the category of literature these days, and literature, according to current norms, is something to which social scientists do not need to pay attention. Sociologists, for example, do not view literature as a source of ideas or as an enterprise that in some ways parallels that of their own, and the reason for this is that they define themselves as scientists in the positivistic tradition; they are not authors, but scientists. Wolf Lepenies and others have pointed out that writing too well is dangerous for a social scientist (since she becomes seen as an author), but they have failed to note that it is not only *how* a sociologist writes but also *what* is being said that separates today's literary authors from the social scientists (e.g. Lepenies 1988). This means that modern social scientists cut themselves off from authors – who are much more ambitious when it comes to covering different aspects of human existence as well as its complexities and contradictions.

The second reason why someone like La Rochefoucauld is ignored by social scientists today is that he wrote in the 1600s or well before there was anything called social science. To use this type of argument, however, ignores the fact that sharp observations of people and their interactions have existed long before the birth of social science. Karl Popper, for example, discusses what he terms 'Plato's sociology' in *The Open Society*; and this is just one example among many that even if the term 'sociology' did not exist before the nineteenth century, sociological reflections certainly did (Popper 1962: 35 ff.).

The general context within which La Rochefoucauld's *Maxims* (1665) was produced is that of an aristocracy situated somewhere between the king and the oppositional Jansenist movement in seventeenth-century France (e.g. Heilbron 1998). La Rochefoucauld was a disillusioned opponent of absolutism, and he often mixed with the Jansenists in the literary salon that he frequented. The Jansenists were part of the Counter Reformation and had developed a religious worldview based on Saint Augustine's ideas that while life in heaven was dominated by God's love, life on earth was dominated by love for oneself or interest. To live a truly virtuous life in this world was impossible, and this meant that behind the humility there was often pride, sin and other manifestations of self-love or interest (*amour-propre*).

According to the standard interpretation of La Rochefoucauld, he essentially secularized the view of the Jansenists and further elaborated on the ways that self-love or interest was at the root of human behaviour. His maxims were penned with much ingenuity; and according to Nietzsche, La Rochefoucauld was one of those 'skillfull marksmen who hit the bull's eye again and again – the bull's eye of human nature' (Nietzsche 1986: 32).

As will soon be shown, the form that La Rochefoucauld chose to use also made it possible for him to make his observations on the role of human behaviour without sacrificing its sometimes paradoxical and contradictory character. He also notes in the preface to the authoritative fifth edition of *Maxims* that he was working with different types of interest: 'the word *Interest* (*intérêt*) does not always mean the interest concerned with material goods, but most often means the interest concerned with glory or honor' (La Rochefoucauld 2001: 2).

What is considered to be one of La Rochefoucauld's most beautiful maxims reads as follows: 'Virtues lose themselves in self-interest, as rivers lose themselves in the sea' (La Rochefoucauld 2001: 33). In the first half of this maxim, the sharp line between virtue and self-interest has been effaced, and it is hinted that virtue may in reality be, or it may become, something quite different from what it aspires to be. In the second half of the sentence the reader is provided with a metaphor (rivers losing themselves in the sea) that sharpens the thought in the first half and also adds to it. It is now suggested that virtue and self-interest may in fact be the same (both consist of water), and that the role of virtue is very small compared to that of self-interest (as small as rivers, compared to the sea).

Another maxim reads as follows: 'Self-interest which is accused of all our crimes often deserves to be praised for our good actions' (La Rochefoucauld 2001: 60). The first half here protests against the common tendency to blame all that is negative on self-interest; self-interest is much too often singled out for critical remarks. In reality things are different. All that is bad is not due to self-interest; and some of what is good may also come from self-interest. Good and bad, in brief, may both originate in self-interest.

The same contradictory and paradoxical quality of self-interest is also characteristic of another maxim: 'Self-interest, which blinds some, brings enlightenment to others' (La Rochefoucauld 2001: 10). A person who is greedy, for example, may lose sight of what she really wants. But interest may also make a person concentrate and focus, and thereby muster the intellectual capacity and energy to accomplish something. In this case, self-interest allows the individual to reach her goal.

Finally, La Rochefoucauld sums up many of his ideas about interest in the following maxim: 'Self-interest speaks all manner of tongues and plays all manner of roles, even that of the disinterested' (La Rochefoucauld 2001: 10). This maxim primarily tells the reader to be sceptical and not take what is being said at face value – and this applies to friendship, politics and business as well as many other contexts. Beneath all of the talk and all of the phrases, you will find an interest. This also goes for the situation when someone explicitly denies that an interest is involved, and presents the whole thing as an example of *disinterest* – say, the result of generosity, love, objectivity and so on.

The Use of Interest in the Scottish Enlightenment (David Hume, Adam Smith)

The step from La Rochefoucauld to David Hume (1711–76) may at first seem large, but France and Scotland were traditional allies and the members of the Scottish elite were familiar with French culture, a fact that is often cited as one of the reasons why the Scottish Enlightenment (*c.* 1740–90) came into being in the first place. The social foundation of this new group was the alliance between the modernizing aristocracy of the Lowlands and the growing middle class in the cities. Another factor in the development of the Scottish Enlightenment was the 1707 Act of Union, through which Scotland was united with England. Through this act, the Scots were suddenly confronted with the new and emerging reality of modern capitalism, and had to take a stance towards it. The Scottish Enlightenment made seminal contributions primarily to history, economics and philosophy and is also credited with having laid the foundation more generally for social science, including sociology.

David Hume embodied the spirit of the Scottish Enlightenment through his empiricism, scepticism and hostility to all forms of superstition. The only solid foundation for philosophy, he argued, was man himself, and he described his philosophy as 'the science of Man' (Hume 1978: xv). What explained the behaviour of human beings was their reason and their passions; and Hume's own ideal can be described as a proper balance between these two in the form of enlightened self-interest. People also interact with one another, and their values as well as interests originate in public opinion.

Interest, according to Hume, is 'entirely governed by *opinion*' or, translated into the language of contemporary sociology, interest is a social construction (Hume 1985: 51).

Interest, as already has been noted, is a central category in Hume's view of what propels human behaviour: 'Nothing is more certain, then that men are, in a great measure, govern'd by interest' (Hume 1978: 534). Hume also regarded justice as based on interest, a view that represents an important innovation in the history of interest. To base justice directly on reason would be futile, according to *A Treatise of Human Nature* (Hume 1978: 490–501). People's sense of benevolence or generosity to one another, he also notes, is similarly much too weak to bear the weight of justice. And to believe that self-interest by itself would lead to justice is an illusion, since chaos would be the result if all individuals simply pursued their own self-interests. Justice must be based on self-interest, Hume argues – but in a way that prevents its destructive potential from being unleashed.

How could this be accomplished? Hume's solution is to use self-interest itself as a way to control or to counter self-interest. 'There is no passion, therefore, capable of controlling the interested affection, but the very affection itself, by an alteration of its direction' (Hume 1978: 492). The way that this can be engineered is if all individuals can be brought to realize that it is in their interest that others respect their interests, and vice versa. Hume works out this argument by using possession as his example since he viewed justice and property as closely related. 'I observe, that it will be for my interest to leave another in possession of his goods, *provided* he will act in the same manner with regard to me' (*ibid.*: 490). Once justice has been introduced through this type of balance of interests, Hume adds, a sense of morality will eventually develop that reflects this situation and also strengthens it.

The concept of interest also plays a key role in Hume's theory of government. One of the tasks of the government is to ensure justice; and justice cannot be left to people's own doings since this would lead to anarchy. There has to be 'an universal and inflexible observance of the rules of justice', and this can only be the case if the administration of justice is assigned to the government (*ibid.*: 534). Also the administration of justice, Hume says, should be based on interest; and this can be accomplished by making it the interest of certain people that justice is indeed created ('with respect to a few, whom we thus immediately interest in the execution of justice' – *ibid.*: 537). While a government is needed for the effective administration of possession and property, there also exist some other cases where it is in everybody's interest that the general interest prevails. As examples of this, Hume mentions the construction of bridges and harbours as well as the organization of the army.

As one would expect, Hume points to the existence of 'violent passions' as one of the reasons why people fail to see the general interest in many situations (*ibid.*: 538). He also devotes a considerable amount of time to discuss another reason for this, namely people's inborn tendency to prefer immediate interests to those that are more distant. People's 'present interests' differ from their 'remote interests', Hume says, and he adds that the latter are typically their true or 'known interests' (*ibid.*: 535, 545).

Hume also ascribes an important role to interest in the way that political power or government should be structured; and he here takes his point of departure in the thesis that 'every man ought to be supposed a *knave*, and to have no other end, in all his actions, than private interest' (Hume 1978: 42). According to Hume, people are much less honest in public or political life than in their private lives, and this must be taken into account in political life or the result will be that separate interests prevail. The solution to this problem, Hume argues, is to be found in the idea that self-interest is not only the major force that drives the individual in public life, but that 'by this interest we must [also] govern him' (*ibid.*: 42). This can be done through a separation of powers or, in Hume's terminology, through 'checks and controls of the constitution' (*ibid.*). What we find here, in other words, is a justification for the separation of powers that draws on the language and imagery of interest.

In his discussion of justice, Hume notes that morals will eventually follow on interests and add to their hold on the individual; and he similarly argues that a government is typically not only based on 'interests' but also on 'right' or what we also may call legitimation (*ibid.*: 33). According to Stephen Holmes in 'The Secret History of Self-Interest', Hume was extremely careful to avoid tautology in his use of self-interest, and he constantly emphasizes that factors other than self-interest are involved. These other factors, according to Hume, are 'the disagreeable passions, fear, anger, dejection, grief, melancholy, anxiety, &c' (Holmes 1990: 270).

Hume also introduces the notion of 'imaginary interest' to account for some of these situations; and he refers to the prevalence of 'vengeance without any regard to interest' (Hume 1978: 63; 1966: 301). In his well-known article on factions, or special interests that have become elevated to general interests, Hume also notes that people can be extremely cruel to one another and kill one another for little or no reason (Hume 1978: 54–63). Holmes summarizes Hume's use of the concept of interest in a non-tautological manner as follows: people's behaviour is not only driven by interest but also by other motives; and each of these two sets of factors can be calculating as well as non-calculating in nature (see Table 1.1).

Through the Scottish Enlightenment the concept of interest was given a central place also in the analysis of the economy, conceived as its own arena or sphere in society. The major figure here is Adam Smith, whose *The Wealth of Nations* (1776) is generally considered to be the first major work in modern economics. Casting Smith in the role of the first modern economist, however, makes it easy to cast him and his work too much in contemporary categories. *The Wealth of Nations* grew out of Adam Smith's lectures as the holder of a Chair in Moral Philosophy in Glasgow, as did *The Theory of Moral Sentiments*. It has increasingly been realized that Adam Smith's main concern was not to lay the foundation for modern economics as much as to find a place for virtue in commercial society, and this effort was also reflected in the use that he made of the concept of interest (e.g. Tribe 1999). Smith, like the other members of the Scottish Enlightenment, saw himself first and foremost as a moral philosopher.

Table 1.1 David Hume's use of the concept of interest, according to Stephen Holmes

	Interest	Other motives
Calculating	1	2
Non-calculating	3	4

Note: Stephen Holmes argues that Hume was always very careful to show that not only interest but also other motives must be part of what explains human behaviour or the analysis will become tautological. This table, which was suggested to Holmes by Albert O. Hirschman, illustrates how Hume tried to avoid tautology as well as explanations in terms of simple dichotomies.

Source: Stephen Holmes (1990: 538, n. 12)

In order to accomplish anything of an economic nature, we read in *The Wealth of Nations*, human beings must cooperate. This can in principle only be done in two ways: by relying on the benevolence of other people, and by somehow inducing others to cooperate by appealing to their 'self-love' or 'interest'. The benevolence of others, however, does not go very far, according to Smith, and only beggars rely on it. Indeed, not even beggars rely on it all the time since they also use money. To cite one of the most familiar sections in *The Wealth of Nations*:

> But man has almost constant occasion for the help of his brethren, and it is in vain for him to expect it from their benevolence alone. He will be more likely to prevail if he can interest their self-love in his favor ... It is not from the benevolence of the butcher, the brewer, or the baker, that we expect our dinner, but from their regard to their interest. (Smith 1976: 26 7)

You can appeal to the interest of other people in three different ways, according to *The Wealth of Nations*. You can either buy something from someone ('purchase'); or you can exchange something ('barter'); or you can come to an agreement ('treaty') (*ibid*: 27). Smith argues that these three ways of appealing to the interest of other people all come naturally to human beings, while 'the propensity to truck, barter and exchange one thing for another' is unknown among animals (*ibid*.: 25).

It is also this propensity that drives the division of labour; and it was Adam Smith's firm conviction that it was the division of labour that accounted for the wealth of a country. While immensely beneficial to humanity in this sense, the division of labour was, however, also destructive since it had a negative impact on certain groups of people. Workers in particular suffered from an advanced division of labour in the factories since this made them 'as stupid and ignorant as it is possible for a human being to become' (*ibid*.: 782). To counter these negative effects of interest-driven behaviour, Smith says, the government must take action.

The Wealth of Nations contains a famous critique of mercantilism, in which the concept of interest plays an important role as well. Different groups have different economic interests, and in mercantilism 'the interest of the producer' has been given precedence over 'the interest of the home-consumer' (*ibid*.: 660). Indeed, mercantilism came into being as a result of the interests of the producers, with merchants and manufacturers being its 'principal architects' (*ibid.*: 661). Mercantilism also implied a much too interventionist government for Smith's taste; and he cites the proverb that once a rod is bent one way, you must bend it the other way to get it straight. This means that in order to correct for the privileges that some groups have been granted, you have to compensate others, and so on.

In contrast to the highly regulated life that characterizes mercantilism, Smith wanted a society based on a 'system of natural liberty' (*ibid.*: 687). The basic rule of conduct for the individual in this system he described as follows: 'Every man, as long as he does not violate the laws of justice, is left perfectly free to pursue his own interest his own way, and to bring both his industry and capital into competition with those of any other man, or order of men' (*ibid.*: 687). The government will have to give up the interventionist power it has in mercantilism and limit itself to the following tasks: to uphold law and order; to defend the country; and to guarantee a minimal level of education and infrastructure ('the three duties of the sovereign') (*ibid.*).

The Wealth of Nations also contains an analysis of the use of interest as an incentive. According to Smith, 'it is the interest of every man to live as much at his ease as he can'; and this means that if he is paid the same for performing some difficult task as for not performing it, he will choose to do the latter (*ibid.*: 760). In settings such as a university, for example, deals are often struck to the effect that individuals will allow everybody else to neglect their duties, on condition that the others let them do the same. Adam Smith also applied his theory of interests as incentive to the category of clergymen. Here, however, he argued that the point was *not* to relate the task of conversion to the salary – or the result would be a much too zealous clergy.

No account of Adam Smith's view of interests is complete without a mention of his ideas about the invisible hand, so a few words need to be said on this topic. The reason why I have not addressed it earlier is that the invisible hand plays a very small role in Smith's work, while posterity has elevated it into *the* main thesis of *The Wealth of Nations*. Indeed, the expression 'the invisible hand' occurs only once in this work and quite far into the text (*ibid.*: 456). The metaphor is used, first of all, to convey the idea that while the individual only seeks his own interest, he will in reality be furthering the general interest at the same time: 'he intends only his own gain, and he is in this, as in many other cases, led by an invisible hand to promote an end which was no part of his intention' (*ibid.*). But Smith also takes the chance to argue that people who try to promote the general interest in a conscious manner, often do worse in furthering this general interest than if they had just stuck to their individual interest. 'I have never known much good done by those who affected to trade for the public good' (*ibid.*).

The Use of Interest by the Utilitarians (Bentham, Mill)

The two central ideas in utilitarianism is that the moral value of an act is directly related to its consequences ('utility'), and what is considered good is always rooted in 'pleasure', just as what is bad is rooted in 'pain'. The concept of interest is often used by the utilitarians, and one may definitely speak of an elective affinity between this type of thought and the interest tradition. Both, for example, tend to reduce a complex reality to another rudimentary terminology; and both were also deeply sceptical of official morality and reality. While the concept of interest and that of utility are by no means identical in the works of Bentham and Mill, they are very close and they would eventually also become identical in late nineteenth-century economics.

As will soon be shown in some detail, the two major proponents of utilitarianism – Jeremy Bentham and John Stuart Mill – thought in terms of interest and often used the term. It is possible to find new and fresh approaches to the concept of interest in their works; one can also learn quite a bit from the way they used it in their analyses. As in La Rochefoucauld, Hume and Smith, there is furthermore the beginning of a social or sociological analysis in the works of the utilitarians that is closely related to the concept of interest. For Bentham, this was mainly expressed in the language of law and legal reasoning, while Mill cast his ideas in the form of 'the moral sciences' and how these differed from the natural sciences ('the exact sciences').

Raymond Boudon and François Bourricaud argue in one of their articles that utilitarianism is not only a philosophical doctrine but also contains 'a complex reflection on the role of interests in social order and social change' (Boudon and Bourricaud 1989: 419). Once this has been said, however, it should also be made clear that the main importance of utilitarianism in the history of the concept of interest is that it initiated the modern tendency to reduce interest to economic interest and to view it in an entirely asocial manner.

Bentham's version of utilitarianism was more radical and consistent than John Stuart Mill's, since he made no exceptions from the idea that everything can be reduced to pleasure and pain. When it came to his use of the concept of interest, this radicalism translated into a belief in Bentham's early work that people are mainly driven by egoism or self-interest. In *The Principles of Morals and Legislation* it is, for example, said that 'the only interest which a man at all times and upon all occasions is sure to find *adequate* motives for consulting, are his own' (Bentham 1948: 313).

But once it has been understood that people are basically propelled by what they regard as their interests, Bentham also notes that people will always take 'the happiness of other men' into account (*ibid.*). By this he means such things as benevolence, actors' concern with their reputation and their desire for friendship. In *The Principles of Morals and Legislation*, in brief, Bentham uses interests in a non-tautological way since actions, from his perspective, are also caused by factors other than interests. He does not, however, elaborate on what he means by interest but basically uses the term in a generic manner.

This way of approach things undergoes a change in Bentham's later work, where we find a multitude of interests, but also a tendency to use interest in a clearly tautological way. This comes out with much clarity in a writing entitled 'Table of the Springs of Action', which represents the most concentrated effort by Bentham to explicate what interests are and what role they play in human affairs. The basic idea is that what causes action (its 'springs of action') are 'pleasures' and 'pains' as well as the 'interests' or 'motives' that correspond to these. No great subtlety of argument can be found in this article, where we read that 'a man is said *to have an interest in any subject*, in so far that *subject* is considered as more or less likely to be to him a source of pleasure or exemption' (Bentham 1843: 207).

In 'Table of the Springs of Action' Bentham enumerates 14 different springs of action as well as the 14 interests that answer to these. Some of Bentham's candidates are quite conventional, such as 'sexual interests', religious interests ('interests of the altar') and economic interests ('pecuniary interests'). Others are more innovative, such as 'interests of the heart' and 'interests of the spying-glass'. The former refers to one's affections for individuals, political communities and mankind as a whole. 'Interests of the spying-glass' refer to a set of phenomena that people today have in mind when they say that they find something *interesting*. Bentham characterizes this phenomenon as follows: '1. Curiosity. 2. Inquisitiveness. 3. Love of novelty. 4. Love of experiment. 5. Desire of information' (Bentham 1843: 199).

While it is true that Bentham's tendency in *The Principles of Morals and Legislation* to equate interest with an undifferentiated concept of self-interest, and that this approach has been replaced by a considerably more elaborate one in 'Table of the Springs of Action', it would also appear that this change has led to a tautological approach. This comes out, for example, in Bentham's discussion of distinterestedness where he says that a disinterested act is impossible. 'In regard to *interest*, in the most extended – which is the original and only strictly proper sense – of the word *disinterested*, no human act ever has been, or ever can be, *disinterested*' (Bentham 1843: 211–12).

John Stuart Mill is well known for his attempt to remove some of the crudest hedonism from Bentham's thought, while respecting its core of utility, pleasure–pain and the greatest happiness principle (that the goal of one's actions should be the greatest happiness for the largest number of people). One well-known example of Mill's attempt to soften Bentham's approach and introduce some idealism into it can be found in 'On Liberty', where Mills famously states that 'I regard utility as the ultimate appeal on all ethical questions; but it must be utility in the largest sense, grounded on the permanent interests of man as a progressive being' (Mill 1961: 264). This statement also points to another tendency in Mill's use of the term 'interest', namely his creative extension of it in several new directions. Among these new directions, the way that Mill used economic interest in his economic writings holds a very special place in the history of the concept of interest, and therefore deserves a special discussion.

Before turning to this topic, however, it may be noted that while Mill assigned an important place to self-interest in his system of thought, he also problematized it and criticized it. There is, according to Mill, 'legitimate' as well as 'illegitimate self-interest'; he also happily pointed out that 'all selfish interests must be terminated by death' (Mill 1961: 354–55; Holmes 1990: 344). His rejection of a tautological use of interest is, for example, clear from his argument that the actions of rulers cannot be exclusively explained by their interests; you also have to take their sense of duty, attitude to tradition and philanthropy into account.

One can in addition find a creative use of the idea that there exist different types of interest in Mill's thought. As an example of this, one can mention his discussion of men's versus women's interests in a parliamentary debate that took place in 1867. The reader may also want to pay attention to Mill's observation that one group of people may in certain situations represent the interests of another group:

> The interests of all women are safe in the hands of their fathers, husbands, and brothers, who have the same interest with them, and not only know, far better than they do, what is good for them, but care much more for them than they care for themselves. Sir, this is exactly what is said of the unrepresented classes. The operatives, for example: are they not virtually represented by the representation of their employers? Are not the interests of the employers and that of the employed, when properly understood, the same? ... And, generally speaking, have not employers and employed a common interest against all outsiders, just as husband and wife have against all outside the family? And what is more, are not all employers good, kind, benevolent men, who love their workpeople, and always desire to do what is most for their good? All these assertions are as true, and as much to the purpose, as the corresponding assertions respecting men and women. (Mill 1988: 150)

In the long run, however, there is no doubt that Mill's most seminal contribution to the way that the concept of interest has been used in modern thought can be found in his economics. Mill is generally considered to be the father of the idea of *homo economicus* or the theory that when you analyse economic phenomena, the assumption must be made that what drives the actor is one and only one thing, namely economic interest.

Mill drew up the main lines for this type of approach in his essay 'On the Definition of Political Economy; and on the Method of Investigation Proper to It' (1836). He here states that in order to turn political economy into a true science, you have to make the assumption that 'the pursuit of wealth' is the only thing that drives man's behaviour in economic matters and 'that man is a being who is determined, by the necessity of his nature, to prefer a greater portion of wealth to a smaller in all cases' (Mill 1992: 137–9). Mill finishes his argument as follows: 'Not that any political economist was ever so absurd as to suppose that mankind really are thus constituted, but because this is the mode in which science must necessarily proceed' (*ibid.*: 139).

Concluding Comments

The main point of this chapter has been to show that there exist many different traditions of thought in which the concept of interest has played an important role, and that this contributes to its richness. What unites all of these traditions is that they (1) use the concept of interest to penetrate deeper into human behaviour; (2) use the concept of interest in a very flexible manner; and (3) apply the concept of interest to a number of very different phenomena.

The way that the concept of interest was used during its first few centuries of existence allowed the analyst to burrow beneath the surface, down to deeper causes. With its help it became possible to see beyond appearances, to make sense of puzzling phenomena and what at first seemed to be paradoxical or contradictory phenomena. The concept of interest, as it appeared during this period, had some of the qualities of a razor: it cut deeply and to the core.

There was also a considerable flexibility to the concept of interest during this time, which no doubt contributed to its popularity. It could, for example, be applied to conscious as well as unconscious motivation. And not only individuals could be assigned interests, but also groups and whole nations. Interests might also differ according to whether they were religious, political, economic, sexual and so on.

And, finally, interest has been used over the centuries to analyse a series of very different phenomena. La Rochefoucauld, for example, used interest to make sense of people's interactions and to analyse moral behavior. Bentham and Mill similarly used interest as the foundation for a moral philosophy. David Hume developed a whole theory of justice as well as a theory of government based on interest. And Adam Smith and John Stuart Mill applied the idea of interest to the sphere of the economy, and in doing so laid the foundation for modern economics. This last achievement brings us to the next chapter, in which the economists' concept of interest as well as that of some early social thinkers constitute the focus.

2

Interest Becomes a Social Science Concept

The basic message of the first chapter in this book is, to repeat, that the concept of interest has several rich traditions on which to draw, and that during the period from around 1500 to the early 1800s it was used to explain a number of very different phenomena. While this flexibility of the concept of interest should be seen as one of its strengths, there is also the fact that it is confusing to see how many different meanings have been attributed to the concept of interest. One feels a bit like the reader of one of Borges' stories in which the reader is told that according to 'a certain Chinese encyclopedia', animals are divided into the following categories:

> (a) those that belong to the Emperor, (b) embalmed ones, (c) those that are trained, (d) suckling pigs, (e) mermaids, (f) fabulous ones, (g) stray dogs, (h) those that are included in this classification, (i) those that tremble as if they are mad, (j) innumerable ones, (k) those drawn with a very fine camel's hair brush, (l) others, (m) those that have just broken a flower vase, (n) those that resemble flies from a distance. (Borges 1964: 103)

But even if it is true there is a certain embarrassment of riches to the study of the concept of interest, there do exist some common structural features to its multiple meanings and uses. Albert O. Hirschman talks, to recall, of 'the interest paradigm', but I prefer to formulate it somewhat differently, namely that there does exist a certain coherence and similarity to the many meanings with which the concept of interest has been invested, during its multiple uses in Western thought (Hirschman 1986: 46). Interest, I would also argue, can perhaps be better described as a concept that is used in many different approaches and traditions – a cross-cutting concept, so to speak – than as a paradigm in the conventional, Kuhnian meaning of this term. In the works of La Rochefoucauld, Hume and so on, the concept of interest may have played an important role – but in no case did it become the foundation for a full philosophy or way of looking at the world. Its ultimate significance in each case was instead determined by its place in a particular system of thought.

The main point in this chapter will be to show how the concept of interest underwent some fundamental changes during the mid- to late nineteenth century, as part of the emergence of modern social science, in particular economics. In order to capture these changes, it is important to first determine what the concept of interest looked like before these changes took place, and this will briefly take us back one last time to La Rochefoucauld and some of the other figures discussed in Chapter 1. I will argue that all of these early thinkers were more or less united in their view of the concept of interest as simultaneously describing (1) a force that helped to account for the actor's behaviour; (2) a force that came from inside the actor; and (3) a force in which important significance was attached to the difference between the existence of the force and the actor becoming aware of its existence. Some of these thinkers were also worried about what would happen if all the individual actors behaved according to their interest, and how this situation should be handled.

Each of these points deserves to be enlarged upon. Before doing so it may be noted that together these points add up to a general theory of what interest is. While I have suggested that it may not be such a good idea to argue that interest is a paradigm of its own, and have argued that it is better described as a cross-cutting concept and a concept used in many different approaches, this is about as close to 'an interest paradigm' as we will come from my perspective.

First of all, then, interest was, during its first few centuries of existence, seen as a major force in accounting for the behaviour of the actor. This meant, on the one hand, that if you could locate the interest of the actor, then you had also succeeded in laying bare one of the major forces that propelled her behaviour (be it the actor herself who did this or an outside observer). Once this has been said, however, it should immediately also be added that these early thinkers had a tendency to use interest in a non-tautological manner, by also attributing explanatory power to forces other than interest. One of these was passions or, as we would say today, emotions.

Secondly – and simultaneously – interest was conceived as being an internal force, that is, as coming from inside the actor. Early thinkers were well aware that there also existed forces *outside* the actor that affected her behaviour as well, such as nature, customs and powerful rulers. These, however, were rather seen as adding to the final form of the actor's behaviour than as her 'springs of action', as Bentham put it. Another consequence of conceiving interest as an internal force was a merger of two ideas that should be kept apart for analytical purposes: interest as a driving force and – since it originates from inside the actor – interest as a force that also expresses what the actor really wants.

The merger of these two ideas also helps to explain the third feature that is characteristic of the early and 'pre-social' form of the concept of interest, namely that there was typically an assumption about a tension between the existence of an interest, on the one hand, and the actor being aware of this interest, on the other. Once the actor became conscious of what her interest was, she would be in a position to realize her innermost wishes. And from this follows the great importance that was traditionally attributed to awareness and insight when it comes to interests.

Finally, several of the thinkers who used the concept of interest were troubled by the fact that it might be dangerous if everybody acted on their interests. That the private interests or self-interests of individual actors were separate from the common interests of all was soon realized. Hobbes famously motivated the existence of a sovereign with the argument that there would be chaos and civil war if everybody acted on their self-interest. Hume similarly argued for a constitutional separation of powers, on the ground that if everybody acted on their interest, all political power might end up in the hands of a single actor. Adam Smith's invisible hand and Mandeville's quip about private vices and public morals were similarly part of a realization among many persons that things would go wrong if everybody acted on their interest.

The rest of this chapter is devoted to an account of what happened to this early view of the concept of interest during the rise of the social sciences in the nineteenth century, especially economics and the early type of sociology that Marx and Tocqueville represent. Economics used the traditional concept of interest to lay the foundation for modern economics and, in the process of doing so, changed it in profound ways. Marx and Tocqueville changed the concept of interest in a different direction, which would be continued and accentuated in academic sociology (as discussed in Chapter 3).

Interest as a Social Science Concept, Part I: Economics

Of all the social sciences, there is none that seized on the concept of interest in such a decesive manner as modern economics. The concept of interest, in all brevity, became the foundation for modern economics; and Pareto's description of economics as 'a general science of interests' is indeed a fit description (Pareto [1916] 1968: 1350). But while economics made interest into its most important concept during the nineteenth century and drew heavily on it for its continued success, it also transformed the concept of interest in the process. It turned it into economic self-interest; and no other types of interest than economic interest (such as political interest, ideal interest, and so on) were referred to in the analysis. The economists transformed interest in a social direction, but it focused on a rather odd and abstract type of social interactions, namely those that make up the perfect market.

How this whole process was played out in the nineteenth century is the topic of the next few pages. It should be emphasized that this account only covers the development of one part of economics, namely the analytical part that made its initial appearance in England and later also in other countries. There was especially one competitor to analytical economics that advocated a much more empirical and historical form of economics, the so-called German Historical School. In this latter type of economics the concept of interest was broad in nature and much closer to the type of interest that was discussed in Chapter 1. The analytical approach to economics and the empirical–historical one confronted one another in a bitter academic fight that took place from the 1880s to around 1900. This so-called Battle of the Methods ended up with a devastating defeat for the empirical–historical type of economics, which from now on was pushed out of economics.

The history of the birth of modern analytical economics in the nineteenth century is complex and difficult to summarize in a few pages. None the less, it is clear that this process began with the realization that economics had to be strictly analytical in its approach and focus exclusively on the economy, as opposed to society as a whole and the role of the economy within this whole.

This step was first taken by John Stuart Mill and David Ricardo, and resulted in a series of ideas for how to proceed that are usually referred to as the theory of *homo economicus*. 'The first principle of Economics is that every agent is actuated only by self-interest', as Edgeworth later was to put it ([1881] 2003: 16). Economic Man is a figure that non-economists like to ridicule and which also seems to have little to do with the sophisticated notions of modern economics. This, however, is not the case, and *homo economicus* is still very much alive in the sense that it still constitutes the foundation of modern economics (e.g. Persky 1995: 221).

According to Kenneth Arrow, the classical description of *homo economicus* can be found in *Risk, Uncertainty and Profit* (1921) by Frank Knight (Arrow 1987: 203). Before presenting Knight's ideas on this topic, however, there is another account of *homo economicus* which deserves to be discussed. This account is much more stylized and to the point than Knight's, and the concept of interest therefore appears with considerably more clarity.

Also this second account is by an economist, but one who is better known for his work in another social science, namely sociology. This is Max Weber, and in his lectures from the 1890s (which are little known), one can find the following succinct statement about what characterizes *homo economicus*:

> Abstract [economic] theory
> a. *ignores*, treats as if *not present* all those motives which have an influence on real men which are specifically *non-economic*, i.e. all those motives not arising from the satisfaction of material needs;
> b. *imputes* as actually present in men particular qualities which are either *not* present or incompletely, namely
> a) complete insight into the given *situation* – perfect economic knowledge;
> b) exclusive selection of the *most appropriate means* for a given end – absolute 'economic rationality';
> c) exclusive devotion of one's own *powers* to the attainment of economic goods – tireless economic endeavor.
>
> It therefore argues on the basis of *unrealistic* men, analogous to a mathematical ideal. (Weber [1898] 1990: 30)

Weber's statement is clear enough, but a few items deserve to be highlighted. First of all, Weber starts out by stating that economics should proceed as if economic action is *exclusively* caused by economic interest ('motive arising from the satisfaction of material needs'). This means that non-economic interests are not taken into account in this type of analysis, either in the area of the economy or in society at large (which is disregarded in the analysis).

The analytical economist, Weber continues, also assumes that the economic actor has knowledge about everything that happens in the economy and knows exactly what her own economic interest is. To this Weber adds that the economic actor also has perfect knowledge about the best way to realize her interest and is committed to doing so. In current language, what Weber is talking about is referred to as 'rational choice' (although 'choice' may be a too strong word since perfect knowledge and transitivity eliminate much of what makes a choice into a choice). Weber concludes by stating that *homo economicus* is, of course, an '*unrealistic* man, analogous to a mathematical ideal'.

What Frank Knight says in *Risk, Uncertainty and Profit* is on the whole the same as Weber – but he lacks Weber's capacity to succinctly summarize what characterizes *homo economicus* in a few sentences, as well as Weber's capacity to make irrational phenomena sound rational. To describe Economic Man, Knight needs fifteen points and five pages, as opposed to Weber's four points and one third of a page. Knight's first point reads as follows:

> 1. The members of the society are supposed to be normal human beings in essential respects as to inherited and acquired dispositions, differing among themselves in the ways and to the degrees familiar in a modern Western nation – a 'random sample' of the population of the industrial nations of to-day. (Knight [1921] 1971: 76)

One thing that is interesting about this statement is that it makes clear what Weber would also emphasize in his later work, namely that *homo economicus* is not only rational but rational of the type that is characteristic of the Western tradition. Other hidden assumptions and non-stated reservations in the theory of *homo economicus* abound in Knight's 15-point description. We read, for example, that 'every person is the final and absolute judge of his own welfare and interests' (*ibid.*: 77). No economic actor is allowed to have power (economic or otherwise) over other actors. The society in which *homo economicus* lives is also assumed to only have law-abiding members; there are no criminals and no expenses for contracts and the like (transaction costs). *Homo economicus* also lives in some special kind of space rather than in a society, since the latter does not seem to exist:

> 6. Every member of the society is to act as an individual only, in entire independence of all other persons. To complete his independence he must be free from social wants, prejudices, preferences, or repulsions, or any values which are not manifested in market dealing. (*ibid.*: 78)

A second step toward modern economics was taken during the nineteenth century and is linked to the idea of marginal utility and people such as Menger, Jevons and Walras. While the set of ideas that go under the name of *homo economicus* express the notion that the economic actor has economic interests, and that he knows exactly what these interests are as well as the best way to realize them, the concept of marginal utility says something else. Its main point is that the economic interest of the actor varies with the *intensity* with which the actor desires something, and that this variation can be expressed through a metric.

Carl Menger has summarized the type of reasoning that the idea of marginal utility is based on in a famous table in *Principles of Economics* (1871). Let us assume, Menger says, that the economic actor wants ten different items and that she ascribes first priority to food (I) and fifth priority to tobacco (V). Assume also that the satisfaction of the actor in consuming the first unit of food is 10, and that it then decreases as successive units are consumed to 9, 8, 7 and so on. The first unit of tobacco, on the other hand, gives the actor a satisfaction that begins with 6 and then decreases with one unit in satisfaction for each additional unit of tobacco consumed, just as food (see Table 2.1 on the next page).

A series of assumptions have to be made to construct a table of this type, including that all goods are comparable in terms of the satisfaction that they give and that they can be ranked in a specific order ('transitivity', meaning that if you prefer *a* to *b*, and *b* to *c*, you will also prefer *a* to *c*). What should also be pointed out is that by making these assumptions, be they unrealistic or not, the first half of modern price theory had been invented, namely the demand curve. According to the typical demand curve, the higher the price of a good, the less units of this good will be demanded and vice versa. When the idea of a similar supply curve was added – as Alfred Marshall did in *Principles of Economics* (1890) – the result was an elegant, analytical model for the determination of price.

Table 2.1 Interest as marginal utility

I	II	III	IV	V	VI	VII	VIII	IX	X
10	9	8	7	6	5	4	3	2	1
9	8	7	6	5	4	3	2	1	
8	7	6	5	4	3	2	1		
7	6	5	4	3	2	1			
6	5	4	3	2	1				
5	4	3	2	1					
4	3	2	1						
3	2	1							
2	1								
1									

Note: In marginal utility analysis the interest of an actor in some specific item depends not only on the inherent value of this item to the actor but also on the intensity with which the actor desires the item. The key idea is explained in the following manner by Carl Menger in *Principles of Economics* (1871). Assume that the actor desires or has an interest in ten goods, and that these can be ranked in a transitive manner, starting with good I and ending with good X. The satisfaction of the actor is also assumed to decrease with one unit, for each unit consumed.

Source: Menger ([1871] 1976: 127).

While the price for using *homo economicus* may initially be high – a series of distortions of empirical reality – it should be pointed out that there was also quite a pay-off later in the analysis. This pay-off is most easily seen by contrasting Economic Man on the individual level to what happens on the collective level, according to the analytical economists. On the individual level, to repeat, *homo economicus* is not impressive – but once we move to the collective level things quickly change. It became possible to calculate a price with precision by using the market as the social mechanism that transforms the subjective desires of an individual actor into a social fact on the collective level.

With a model of this type economists could soon also directly relate changes in the reactions of the economic actors to changes in prices ('elasticity', invented by Marshall). The idea of determining a price in this manner was also eventually extended to other parts of economic life than the market for ordinary goods. It then became possible, for example, to determine the price for the use of money, and thereby add to the theory of finance. Economists could also develop a theory for how labour should be priced, and add to the theory of labour markets. In this way, the idea of *homo economicus*, in combination with the idea of marginal utility, became the foundation for modern economics.

In order to determine the view of interest to which these developments in economics led, it is useful to return to what was said at the outset of this chapter. In terms of conceptualizing interest as a force that determines the behaviour of the actor (1), it is clear that the assumption was made in this new type of economics that there is only *one* force that determines the behaviour of the actor, and this is economic interest. Another restriction may be noted, namely that nineteenth-century economics (as opposed to today's economics) only speaks of action in the area of the economy proper.

As to the idea that the force that drives the actor comes from inside the actor (2), it is obvious that this is also the case for nineteenth-century economics. This type of economics does not, however, research this question or otherwise draw on empirical material (as, for example, La Rochefoucauld had done). Instead it *assumes* or rather *assigns* an internal interest to the actor.

Finally, as to the notion that there exists a tension between the existence of an interest and the actor's knowledge of the interest (3), Menger *et al.* make a very radical move. This is to eliminate this tension by making the assumption that the economic actor has total knowledge of her interests. The interest, and the knowledge about the interest, are still conceptualized as two different things – but the idea that one might just as well collapse the two into one single concept, in the form of 'revealed preferences' (Samuelson) is not far away.

What happened to the concept of interest when it became part of modern economics in the nineteenth century has been nicely summed up by Vilfredo Pareto. According to Pareto, as already mentioned, economics can be described as 'a general science of interests' and one that primarily looks at rational phenomena. It analyses interactions in the market, but these are all logical rather than empirical in nature. Sociology, in contrast, deals primarily with irrational phenomena. Interests are analysed in sociology as well – but as part of a world that is deeply irrational and emotional.

Interest as a Social Science Concept, Part II: The Forerunners of Sociology

The story about the way that economics seized on the concept of interest in the nineteenth century, transformed it according to its own needs, and used it in a very successful manner, is well known. This, in contrast, is not the case with the way that the concept of interest was used in sociology, including early sociology or rather the forms that this type of analysis took before academic sociology had come into being. Few attempts have been made to look systematically at the use of interest in the works of the so-called forerunners of sociology during the nineteenth century and how their use is related to the general history of the concept of interest. This is true for Marx but even more so for Tocqueville; and in the works of these two thinkers one can find quite a few interesting sociological uses of the concept of interest, as the following account will try to show.

Interest in the New World, according to Tocqueville

Ever since Raymond Aron in the 1960s included Tocqueville in his famous course on the classics in sociology at the Sorbonne, it has been common to argue that Tocqueville developed a type of analysis that might just as well be called sociological. In this type of literature it has also been noted that 'the category of interest plays a fundamental part in de Tocqueville's sociological analysis' (Boudon and Bourricaud 1989: 421). It is indeed true that the concept of interest plays an important role in Tocqueville's work. None the less, it would also seem that Tocqueville is better characterized as a kind of transitional figure in social science, and that his work is situated somewhere in the grey zone between early social theory and the type of analysis that towards the end of the nineteenth century became known as sociology.

Similarly, Tocqueville's views on interest are situated on both sides of the boundary between the early theories of interest, which were discussed in Chapter 1, and those that are explicitly social. Tocqueville's view of the psychology of the actor and the role that interests play in her actions, are not very different from those that can be found in the works of, say, David Hume and Adam Smith. But there are also parts of Tocqueville's work that are distinctly social in spirit. This is especially clear in *Democracy in America*, where Tocqueville assigns one type of interest to aristocratic society and another to democratic society. Tocqueville does not use the terminology of the sociologists who would succeed him, such as 'social', 'social action', and so on, but his reasoning in his study of the US fits these categories very well.

Each individual, Tocqueville says in *Democracy in America*, is driven by interests – but only up to a point. Other forces drive the individual as well, and Tocqueville refers in shorthand to these in phrases such as 'interests and passions' and 'interests and affections' (e.g. Tocqueville [1835–40] 2000: 46, 76, 80). The reason for referring to this type of expression as being in shorthand, is that if one takes a close look at Tocqueville's argument in *Democracy in America*, it quickly becomes clear that there are several factors that can affect the actor besides emotions ('passions', 'affections'). There are in particular 'ideas', by which Tocqueville roughly means insights, but also such items as public opinion and ideology (e.g. *ibid.*: 158). There are furthermore 'habits' and related phenomena (*ibid.*: 352).

The concept of habits is close to that of customs, which is a category that points to forces that are beyond the individual, and in this sense are social and non-individual in nature. None the less, what is definitely the most social or sociological use of the concept of interest that can be found in Tocqueville's work is in the way that it is used in the conceptual pair aristocracy–democracy, which constitutes the conceptual core of *Democracy in America*. According to Tocqueville, European society started out as an aristocracy some thousand years ago, meaning by this that a small elite of landowning warriors controlled *all* of the resources (economic, political and religious). As society evolved, this elite gradually lost control over these resources – through the Reformation, the decline of the importance of rural property, the rise of a merchant class, and so on. Tocqueville referred to this development as a growth in 'democracy', while a growth in 'social, economic and political equality' would perhaps have been the terminology used today.

While the fact that people had interests was something that was openly accepted in a democracy like the US, according to Tocqueville, it was hidden in an aristocracy. One reason for this was that aristocratic society was structured in such a way that interests did not operate alone; they were deeply embedded in specific relations and emotions and could only be expressed in conjunction with these. This comes out, for example, in Tocqueville's example of how rent for land is paid in an aristocracy versus in a democracy:

> In aristocratic societies, farm rents are discharged not only in money, but in respect, affection, and service. In democratic countries, they are paid only in money ... it is no more than chance that puts the property owner and the tenant farmer in contact [in a democracy]. They are joined for a moment to negotiate the conditions of the contract, and afterwords they lose sight of each other. They are two strangers whom interest brings together and who rigorously discuss between themselves an affair whose sole subject is money. (*ibid.*: 554)

The rule of interest is also less visible in aristocratic society for another reason, and this is that naked interest is looked down upon and not talked about. While aristocrats are well aware of the role of money and material interests, they keep their ideas and strategies for how to realize these interests to themselves. In public, on the other hand, they show disdain and pretend not to be interested in money and money-making; 'they were pleased to profess that it is glorious to forget oneself and that it is fitting to do good without self-interest like God himself' (*ibid.*: 500).

The situation in a democracy such as the US was exactly the opposite, according to Tocqueville. Here interests were openly acknowledged and each individual was assumed to have interests that only she was aware of as well as responsible for. In a democracy, Tocqueville emphasizes, every individual is the judge of her own interests: 'the individual is the best as well as the only judge of his particular interest' (*ibid.*: 62). Tocqueville agrees that the ideas on interest are much coarser in a democracy than in an aristocracy; on the other hand, they are referred to without hypocritical denial. Tocqueville was also of the opinion that as history moved on in the direction of democracy, interest would become the norm: 'one must therefore expect that individual interest will become more than ever the principal if not the unique motive of men's actions; but it remains to know how each man will understand his individual interest' (*ibid.*: 503).

Tocqueville realized well that when all actors pursue their interests, there will be plenty of conflicts. In *Democracy in America* he follows the eighteenth-century tradition of referring to many different types of interests, and this naturally adds to the potential for many types of conflicts as well. As an example of Tocqueville's sensitivity to the possibility for conflict as well as his attempt to use the concept of interest in a non-tautological manner, one can cite the following example:

> Bring together two men of society, give to these two men the same interests and in part the same opinions; if their characters, their enlightenment, and their civilization differ, there are many chances that they will not agree. (*ibid.*: 361)

The centrepiece of Tocqueville's analysis of interest in *Democracy in America* is the so-called doctrine of interest properly understood. By this awkward-sounding phrase, Tocqueville refers to the fact that what makes it possible to avoid a war of all against all in the US is that the average American sees it as being directly in her interest to behave in a moral and decent manner. Americans regard virtue as 'useful', Tocqueville says, and notes that Benjamin Franklin was of the same opinion (*ibid.*: 501). He sums up his argument as follows:

> In the United States it is almost never said that virtue is beautiful. They maintain that it is useful and they prove it every day. American moralists do not claim that one must sacrifice oneself to those like oneself because it is great to do so; but they say boldly that such sacrifices are as necessary to the one who imposes them on himself as the one who profits from them. (*ibid.*: 501)

By believing that one must be virtuous in order to reach one's goals, many causes for discord are removed. But according to Tocqueville there is also another interesting effect of behaving in this manner, and this is that the individual becomes more disciplined. By saying no to 'a thousand little everyday passions' the individual will not only be in a better position to realize her long-term and permanent interests, but her personality will also change in a rational direction (*ibid.*: 503). Tocqueville's argument on this point is similar to that of Max Weber in *The Protestant Ethic and the Spirit of Capitalism*, where it is suggested that a certain type of religion will make behaviour more rational and methodical, and that this rationality may then migrate to the actor's economic behaviour. Tocqueville takes this last step as well and states that it is the doctrine of self-interest properly understood that constitutes 'the great secret of succeeding in this [world]' (*ibid.*: 522). 'All that elevates, enlarges, extends the soul', he writes in *Democracy in America*, 'renders it more capable of succeeding in the very one of its undertakings that does not concern it' (*ibid.*: 522).

But even if Tocqueville was of the opinion that religion intervened and greatly softened the impact of every individual trying to realize her individual interests, he was none the less worried and also repelled by the cult of interest in the US. Tocqueville's personal distaste for the US in this respect is clear from the following statement: 'one can conceive of nothing so small, so dull, so filled with miserable interests, in a word, so antipoetic, as the life of man in the United States' (*ibid.*: 461).

Tocqueville was also worried on other grounds about the project in democracies of building a society on the basis of openly acknowledged interests and little else. He wondered, for example, if American nationalism – a nationalism that was based directly on interests, as he saw it – could really withstand strong pressure (*ibid.*: 358). The American system of justice was similarly operated via interests and, again, Tocqueville wondered if this was really enough or if a stronger sense of justice was not needed (*ibid.*: 461).

Tocqueville's most serious doubts about the future of a democratic and interest-based society, such as the US, can be found in his argument about 'individualism' (*ibid.*: 482–8). What Tocqueville had in mind with this expression was the danger to which an 'exaggerated love of self' might lead; and he was in particular worried about the political consequences of individualism (*ibid.*: 482). When individuals focus too much on their own interests, he noted, they often come to feel that since they cannot influence politics, they might just as well withdraw into the narrow circle of family and friends and forget about the rest of the world (*ibid.*: 482). As a result, politics will suffer and the door will be opened up to a new kind of oppression that is typical for democracies, namely a soft and mild type of tyranny. In the long run, prosperity will also end since there can be no wealth without virtuous behaviour. Tocqueville sums up his argument by saying that while self-interest is very, very old, there exists a new type of self-interest that can only be found in democracies:

> selfishness is a vice as old as the world. It scarcely belongs to one form of society than to another. Individualism is of democratic origin and it threatens to develop as conditions become equal. (*ibid.*: 483)

Interest in the Old World, according to Marx

Like Tocqueville, Marx's thinking was to a large extent formed by the eighteenth century, and this goes for its content as well as its form. Marx, in all brevity, was very familiar with the works of Adam Smith, David Hume, and so on, and also the way in which they used the concept of interest. As opposed to Tocqueville, however, Marx primarily applied the concept of interest to the Old World, that is, to Europe with its strong heritage of feudalism or 'aristocracy'. While there were no classes (including oppressed classes) in a democracy like the US, according to Tocqueville, one of Marx's great discoveries was precisely that there are classes and that the oppressed have their own interests. Finally, while Tocqueville never developed a closed system in his social theory, Marx eventually did. And the more closed Marx's system became, as we soon shall see, the more he also tended to replace existing categories of thought, including the concept of interest, with categories of his own making.

Before tracing the main steps in Marx's thought, and the place that interest holds in his general system, a few words must be said about the one piece of Marx's writing in which the concept of interest is absolutely at the centre. This is one of his earliest writings, 'Debates on the Law on Thefts of Wood' (1842). Marx would later say that this article grew out of his experience as a journalist and being 'in the embarrassing position of having to discuss what is known as material interest' (Marx [1859] 1970: 19). As we shall see, the article on the law on thefts is so filled with sharp and engaging observations on the role of the concept of interest that it deserves to be known as an important contribution to the literature on interests in its own right.

'Debates on the Law on Thefts of Wood' consists of a series of newspaper articles that Marx wrote in the early 1840s for *Rheinische Zeitung* in response to the decision by the Rhine Province Assembly in 1841 to criminalize the collection of wood in the forest. Poor people had by tradition been allowed to take twigs and branches and use these as fuel, and this customary right was now being revoked. The local warden, who was paid by the owner of the forest, was also assigned the task of overseeing the new law. Marx was infuriated by the new law, and his writings on it have all the bite and sarcasm that is characteristic of his later work.

The main thrust of Marx's argument is that by making material interest into its main concern, the Assembly had deeply degraded the law. The state, as Marx saw things at this stage of his development, should be above all actors or, rather, it should defend all actors in their capacity as citizens and human beings – but definitely not in their capacity as bearers of material interest. If the state makes interest into its leading principle, people will lose their respect for the law, according to Marx. By giving in to the special interest of the forest owner, the Assembly had betrayed its task:

> interest by its very nature is blind, immoderate, one-sided; in short, it is lawless natural instinct, and can lawlessness lay down laws? Private interest is no more capable of legislating by being installed on the throne of the legislator than a mute is made capable of speech by being given an enormously long speaking-trumpet. (Marx [1842] 1975: 261)

Marx's use of the concept of interest in analysing law differs from the equivalent attempts in the works of Hume and Tocqueville, where the main point is rather that interests can be used for the administration of justice. By making it into someone's interest to see to it that the general interest prevails, the general interest will prevail. Marx, on the other hand, makes an argument that material interests represent a threat to justice; they undermine justice and they pervert it. This is particularly the case if material interests are satisfied at the expense of the poor and not regulated according to morality and higher principles.

Marx's article, however, contains much more than his argument against letting interest become the leading principle in the law. Marx tries, for example, to outline the world-view of self-interest ('the world outlook of self-interest'), and it is this attempt that makes this article so special (*ibid.*: 242). Some of Marx's statements on this theme are written with great economy and have the sound and feel of maxims. We read, for example, that 'interest does not think, it calculates' (*ibid.*: 249).

There is also Marx's statement that 'interest has no memory, for it thinks only of itself' (*ibid.*: 247). He adds, 'And the *one* thing about which it [interest] is concerned, itself, it never forgets' (*ibid.*). Marx's final verdict reads as follows: '[Interest] is not concerned about contradictions, for it never comes into contradiction with itself. It is a constant improviser, for it has no system, only *expedients*' (*ibid.*).

Marx also notes how flexible the notion of self-interest is: if it wants to be positive, it can be positive; if it needs to be critical, it can be that as well. Indeed, there is not one world-view of interest but two: 'We see that selfishness has a double set of weights and measures for weighing and measuring people, and two world outlooks, two pairs of spectacles, one showing everything black and the other in rosy tints' (*ibid.*: 242). In a sentence that gives associations to his later critique of bourgeois ideology, Marx adds that 'when it is a matter of making other people the victim of its tools and giving a favourable appearance to dubious means, selfishness puts on its rose-coloured spectacles which impart an imaginary glory to these tools and means, and deludes itself and others with the unpractical, delightful dreaming of a tender and trusting soul' (*ibid.*). But interest does not only see the world in rosy colours; it also knows how to scrutinize things in order to gauge their exact value: 'Like an experienced horse-dealer it subjects people to a lengthy ocular inspection, overlooking no detail, and they seem to it to be as petty, as pitiful, and as dirty, as selfishness itself' (*ibid.*).

That Marx was well aware of the way that the concept of interest had been used by various eighteenth-century thinkers is also clear from some other writings than the youthful article on the law on thefts of wood. In *The Eighteenth Brumaire of Louis Bonaparte*, for example, one can find the following statement, which could just as well have been written by Adam Smith:

> As in private life one differentiates between what a man thinks of himself and says of himself and what he really is and does, so in historical struggles one must still more distinguish the language and the imaginary aspirations of parties from their real organism and their real interests, their conception of themselves from their reality. (Marx [1852] 1978: 128)

Marx also used the concept of interest as part of his enterprise to criticize bourgeois economics and its categories. In *Economic and Philosophical Manuscripts of 1844* Marx states, for example, that political economy takes far too much for granted and avoids giving explanations why certain phenomena exist in the first place. 'When, for example, it [political economy] defines the relationship of wages to profit, it takes the interest of the capitalist to be the ultimate cause, i.e., it takes for granted what it is supposed to explain' (Marx 1964: 106). In *Grundrisse*, written many years later, Marx similarly argues that self-interest is not something that can simply be assumed; the social conditions under which it has come into being also need to be carefully explicated: 'self-interest is itself a socially determined interest and can only be realized within the bounds set by society; it is, in other words, tied to the reproduction of these conditions and means' (Neuendorff 1973: 110).

While Marx deserves a place in the history of the concept of interest for a number of reasons, it is clear that his name is first and foremost associated with one special term that he introduced, and that is *class interest*. While earlier thinkers had sometimes referred to the interests of various groups, the main (and implicit) meaning of their use of group interest was more or less as the aggregated sum of the individual interests of its members. This, however, is not true for class interest in the sense that Marx used it. This concept indicates, in contrast, a reality that has a distinct existence well beyond that of its individual members; and it is thoroughly social in this sense. This is also true for the *strength* of a class. Once the members of a class realize that they are not only isolated individuals ('class-in-itself'), but members of a distinct class with all that this entails ('class-for-itself'), the class is in a position to act with new and superior force.

The basic idea behind the notion of class interest is spelled out as follows in *The Poverty of Philosophy*:

> Economic conditions had first transformed the mass of the people of the country [England] into workers. The combination of capital has created for this mass a common situation, common interests. This mass is thus already a class as against capital, but not yet for itself. In the struggle, of which we have noted only a few phases, this mass becomes united, and constitutes itself as a class for itself. The interests it defends become class interests. But the struggle of class against class is a political struggle.
> (Marx [1847] 1955: 150)

The progression between these two steps – from one that is primarily economic in nature to one that is political – would, however, turn out to be anything but mechanical, as Marx quickly realized. This is especially clear from his analyses of France in the mid-nineteenth century, especially from the way that the peasant class responded to the *coup d'état* of Napoleon III in 1851. Since they did not realize that Napoleon III represented interests antagonistic to their own, the French peasants did not react to the seizure of power. The reason for this passivity, according to Marx, had much to do with the fact that the French peasants were more or less self-sufficient and did not cooperate with one another:

> The small peasants form a vast mass, the members of which live in similar conditions, but without entering into manifold relations with one another. Their mode of production isolates them from one another, instead of bringing them into mutual intercourse. (Marx [1852] 1978: 108)

Marx compares the French peasants to 'a sackful of potatoes' and concludes that since 'the identity of their interests begets no unity' they cannot enforce their class interest (*ibid.*).

While this is not the place to discuss the way that Marxists have picked up on Marx's concept of class interest and transformed it in various ways, something needs to be said about the concept of objective class interest in Marxist thought. A celebrated formulation of this latter concept (which is closely related to Marx's own notion of class-for-itself) can be found in *History and Class Consciousness* by Georg Lukács. According to the argument in this work, the social position of the modern proletariat is unique in that it is the first class in history that has an objective interest in the 'totality' of society, since it aims to liberate all of mankind. According to Lukács:

> By relating consciousness to the whole of society it becomes possible to infer the thoughts and feelings which men would have in a particular situation if they were *able* to assess both it and the interests arising from it in their impact on immediate action and on the whole structure of society. That is to say, it would be possible to infer the thoughts and feelings appropriate to their objective situation. (Lukács [1923] 1971: 51)

While this argument about 'false consciousness' and its abolition was to inflame the imagination of many Marxist intellectuals, it has been of little relevance for Marxist politics since Lukács combined it with a strong advocacy of the Leninist type of party. According to Lenin, workers could by themselves only attain 'trade union consciousness' and had to be led in their actions by a small cadre of professional revolutionaries. How these latter came to know the 'totality' of society and decide on what was in the interest of the proletariat and what was not, was of little concern to Lenin, who simply described the members of the Bolshevik type of party as experienced in the class struggle, seasoned in the revolutionary struggle, and the like (e.g. Lenin [1902] 1969).

If we now return to Marx's own thought, it is clear that the concept of interest is not only political and sociological in nature for Marx; it also plays a key role in his economic analysis. At the same time it would appear that the concept of interest increasingly came to play an invisible role in his economic theory, not in the sense that Marx eliminated it from his analysis but rather that he replaced it with a new and more differentiated terminology of his own. As a consequence of this, one rarely finds the *word* 'interest' in his economic writings, even if the *idea* is still there.

This tendency can be illustrated by contrasting one of Marx's earliest writings on economics, 'Wage, Labour and Capital' (1849) to *Capital* (1867). In the former, where the concept of interest figures prominently, Marx notes, for example, that 'the interests of capital and the interests of wage labour are diametrically opposed' ([1847] 1977: 220). He also rebutted the proposition that 'the worker has an interest in the rapid growth of capital' with the argument that the worker will always gain less than capital (*ibid.*).

In *Capital*, on the other hand, the concept of interest is basically absent from the economic analysis, which is presented with the help of a new set of terms that Marx had developed in his attempt to better understand the nature of capital (surplus value, variable capital, primitive accumulation, and so on). But it is also possible to find some echoes from the eighteenth-century use of the term 'interest' in *Capital*; and one example of this would be Marx's reference to 'the most violent, mean and malignant passions of the human breast, the Furies of private interest' (Marx [1867] 1906: 15). Marx also makes fun of Adam Smith's idea that private interests do not clash when they are unleashed – but that is about all.

Summing up Marx's use of the concept of interest, one can say that he definitely used it in a sociological sense in his concept of class interest. The term 'class interest' is much more Marx's invention than what 'class' is. In the former concept he also makes a skilful and novel use of the classic tension in the concept of interest between what an interest would appear to be and what it really is ('class-in-itself' versus 'class-for-itself'). The distance between the two is traditionally covered by the actor becoming aware of her interests, but Marx changed this into a huge number of actors becoming aware of their interest in common through interaction with one another.

As to Marx's use of interest as an economic concept, it is clear that this tended to disappear from Marx's vocabulary as he dug deeper into things and needed a more differentiated terminology. A few points, however, deserve to be stressed in this context in order to separate out Marx's use of the concept of interest from that of conventional economics. One is that Marx spoke of the economic interest of the *oppressed*, something that represents a novelty. Another is that he kept the idea of interest as a strong driving force in *Capital*, even if he did not use the term itself. Finally, in Marx's hands interest always implies conflict.

Concluding Remarks

The approach to interest that can be found among the analytical economists in the nineteenth century differed sharply from the one that was dominant among intellectuals in the eighteenth. For one thing, the only type of interest that was taken into account by the analytical economists was economic interest. Secondly, the actor whose action was analysed was restricted to one and only one sphere in society, namely the economy. Thirdly, the actor was assumed to have perfect knowledge of her interest; and the notion that an actor's interest was somehow hidden and had to be located as well as identified before it could be realized, was gone. And lastly, the eighteenth-century psychology of man had been abandoned. Economic Man was pre-psychological in the sense that he had made his appearance before the science of psychology had come into being (e.g. Hirschman 1977). But he was also non-psychological by design, in the sense that the economists explicitly stated that economic analysis did not (and should not) have anything to do with psychology.

Still, there is no doubt that in his own way *homo economicus* was a social being. The place *par excellence* where *homo economicus* could be found was the market, where the price was set through interactions between buyers and sellers. Their contact, however, was truly minimal, and Jevons, Menger, Walras *et al.* all agreed that it also had to remain minimal if their models were to function. Consumers, for example, were not allowed to be influenced by other consumers, just as workers should not unite in trade unions if labour markets were to operate properly. Similarly, nineteenth-century economists were concerned with the collective (or social) outcome of the economic process. They did not, however, take the position that there were opposing and contradictory interests in the economy, but instead followed the lead of Adam Smith and assumed away conflicts of interest.

Also Tocqueville and Marx moved away from the eighteenth-century notion of interest, but in a different direction from that of the analytical economists. They did, on the whole, say farewell to the individual psychology of the eighteenth century, but they also stayed away from the assumption of perfectly homogeneous actors. And if they sometimes wanted to replace the concept of interest, it was to improve it, not to retire it.

As for the individual psychology of the eighteenth century, it is obvious that Marx found no place for it in his work, whereas Tocqueville's position is more ambivalent. Marx paid no attention whatsoever to the psychology of individual actors in the system that he created and explicitly stated that he was only talking of capitalists and workers as types, not as individuals. Tocqueville, in contrast, often refers to 'the interests and the passions' of the individual and was for ideological reasons wedded to a concern with the individual. But even so, it is clear that Tocqueville's treatment of interest in his analysis of democracy versus aristocracy shows that he saw interest as something that was deeply influenced by the social structure, and perhaps even a social construction. Tocqueville also argued that self-interest only exists and can exist in its purity in a democracy.

Tocqueville's notion of self-interest, it should be finally noted, differs from that of Marx in that it is broader and more social in nature. Marx had a tendency to deflate interest to greed and naked self-interest. This can be illustrated by the famous statement in *The Communist Manifesto* that the only link between people in a capitalist society is that of self-interest: 'the bourgeoisie ... has left remaining no other nexus between man and man than naked self-interest, than callous "cash payment"' (Marx and Engels [1848] 1976: 487).

If one makes a quick survey of the use of the concept of interest in the writings by Tocqueville and Marx, in an attempt to establish when they used it in a distinctly social sense, special attention must be paid to the notion of class interest. Marx should also be given credit for having included the idea of *force* – of strong, driving power – in his concept of interest. An oppressed class is made up of a mass of individuals who are all driven by their interests, and when these realize that they have interests in common, according to

Marx, their strength may grow to a storm through which society can be fundamentally changed.

There exists, of course, no equivalent to this in Tocqueville, who anyway argued that classes belong to aristocracies and cannot be found in democracies. Still, Tocqueville was sensitive to the way that individuals in a democracy can unite around their interests and in this way accomplish a host of different tasks. Their tool for doing so was primarily the organization, and *Democracy in America* is filled with praise for the skill with which the Americans knew how to form and run organizations.

Once the topic of forming organizations has been brought up, one also realizes the limits to Marx's vision of the (social) coming together of interests in the idea of class interests. The reason for this is that what primarily counts for Marx is the nearly instinctual realization of workers and other oppressed people that they have interests in common. That they also can form organizations for pretty much anything that they want to accomplish did not concern Marx and is not discussed in his work.

There is finally also the fact that the concept of interest tends to disappear in some types of interest analyses during the nineteenth century. Analytical economists, as especially Albert O. Hirschman has argued, introduced notions such as utility and ophemility in an attempt to make interest into something more acceptable and legitimate. This may well be true, but we are also seeing another tendency in *homo economicus*, namely the attempt to change the meaning of interest from being a strong, driving force to becoming a rational way of making decisions and more generally a way of approaching reality through an analytical approach. What defines economics as a science, twentieth-century economists argue, is not its subject matter but its approach: that it has a special and distinctly rational perspective.

Marx and Tocqueville do not take this route. Instead they take leave of the concept of interest when they need a more differentiated concept. Marx's replacement of 'material interest' with a series of concepts that he found useful to trace the way that profit-making interests are realized through the capitalist process, is a case in point. While Marx and Tocqueville were loath to abandon the *idea* of interest as a driving force in the individual, the economists were not. The stance of the academic sociologists on this issue is one of the topics that will be discussed in the next chapter.

3
Sociologists on Interest

The concept of interest is currently not an accepted sociological concept. It is true that it often appears in sociological writings, and it is also true that if one consults a sociological dictionary there may well be an entry for 'interest' (or 'interests'). But even when the concept of interest does appear in a sociological text or in a sociological dictionary, its meaning is more or less taken for granted and there are no references to its earlier use, to alternative meanings and the like. It is a concept without history and it also presents no problems. It constitutes, in brief, what Robert K. Merton has termed a 'proto-concept' or a term that is used without awareness and conceptual precision – and which for this very reason does not fulfil its function as a social science concept very well. 'A proto-concept is an early, rudimentary, particularized, and largely unexplicated idea', according to Merton, '[while] a concept is a general idea which once having been defined, tagged, substantially generalized, and explicated can effectively guide inquiry into seemingly diverse phenomena' (Merton 1984: 267). In short, when it comes to the sociological concept of interest, everyone has to reinvent the wheel on her own.

It was just pointed out that when the concept of interest is used by contemporary sociologists, no reference is typically made to its earlier use, save perhaps that Marxist sociologists may cite Marx on class interest. One of the purposes of this chapter is therefore to give back to the concept of interest its own history, especially when it comes to its sociological use. As things turn out, a large number of sociologists have drawn on the concept of interest in their work, and the history of these uses is complex and fascinating in its own right. Since it is also a history that is little known today, it deserves to be told so that it can be incorporated into the more general history of the concept of interest.

To write this history in the detail that it deserves, however, is a task that goes beyond the aim of this short book, and it would also take us in a different direction from the one that I want to take, namely to figure out how the concept of interest can be used in a creative way in sociology and social science analysis more generally. Instead of presenting the use of the concept of interest among sociologists in chronological order – starting with the sociological classics and ending today – I have therefore chosen to centre this chapter around the question of whether sociologists, in their attempts to struggle with the concept of interest, have succeeded in coming up with a useful concept.

None the less, a few words do need to be said about the history of the use of the concept of interest in sociology from a more conventional perspective. While there are still many holes to be filled in, the broad outlines of such an account would appear to be the following. The one time during the history of sociology that a serious and concerted effort was made to turn the concept of interest into a sociological concept, and when there was also a lively discussion of its pros and cons, was during its pioneer phase, roughly 1890–1910. The central figure in this effort was Gustav Ratzenhofer (1842–1904), an Austrian sociologist who is largely forgotten today. His ideas were especially well received in the US, where two of the central figures in early American sociology – Albion Small and E.A. Ross – not only felt that the concept of interest deserved to be incorporated into the sociological analysis, but also assigned a central place to it.

The concept of interest was also used by the classics in sociology, and several of them found it extremely useful. This is especially true for Max Weber and Georg Simmel, who both regarded interest as the main driving force in modern society. Weber also attempted to develop several distinct concepts by introducing the concept of interest into them, as exemplified by class, certain types of collective action, and so on. Emile Durkheim was much less enthusiastic about the concept of interest than Weber and Simmel but, none the less, cast some of his most important concerns in the language of general interest versus self-interest. In brief, interest was very much part of the set of ideas that the classics used when they laid the foundation for modern sociology.

Exactly what happened after the classics is not very clear, except that the way that the concept of interest had been discussed by Ratzenhofer and the classics now fell into oblivion. No references to its earlier use were made from then on, and this is still the case.

The general verdict appears to have been that interest was part of the general social science vocabulary but did not constitute a sociological concept of its own or otherwise merit much discussion. The classical textbook in sociology by Park and Burgess (1921) basically ignores the concept of interest, while it is directly criticized in *The Structure of Social Action* ([1937] 1968) by Talcott Parsons.

After World War II the concept of interest has occasionally resurfaced, not least in the stratification literature and in exchange theory. Only two of the major sociologists from the post-World War II period, however, have assigned it a central role in their systems, as far as I know. These are two sociologists who otherwise belong to very different camps, namely James Coleman and Pierre Bourdieu.

The ideas on interest by Ratzenhofer, Small, Weber, Coleman and so on all deserve a discussion of their own, especially since their ideas have not been given the attention they deserve. To some extent I will also try to discuss each of them in this chapter. Since the aim of this chapter is to try to establish a useful sociological concept of interest rather than to write its history, I will proceed as follows. I have grouped the ideas of Ratzenhofer and all the other sociologists into a few categories, as a way of starting a discussion of them. In the first of these the concept of interest is seen as being of crucial importance and as *the* major cause or driving force of social behaviour. In the second category, interest is still of much importance, but it is also argued that there are several other forces that cause social behaviour. The third category is about theories that argue that interest is of little or no importance.

Approach 1: Interest as *the* Driving Force in Social Life

Each of the three categories just mentioned should be seen as ideal types in the sense that they will be presented with a conceptual clarity that they lack in reality. It is also the case that some authors fall into several categories, even if the main gist of their thinking usually qualifies them for one rather than another category. The first category to be discussed is the one according to which interest is seen as *the* major cause in social life and consequently of crucial importance to sociological theory. What I will try to do primarily is to show how well the authors who belong to this category are able to argue for their position and if their arguments hold up. It is clear that the position taken by, say, Ratzenhofer and Simmel around 1900 will differ from that of James Coleman, who was active some 50 years later.

In 1905 Albion Small, who was the head of the Department of Sociology at the University of Chicago, noted that 'no single term is of more constant use in recent sociology than this term "interests"' (Small 1905: 434; similarly House 1926: 508). This statement was made in Small's most important work, *General Sociology*. The very same year another pioneer in US sociology, E.A. Ross, published a similarly fundamental work *Foundations of Sociology*, in which interest was also the central category (Ross 1905). And a few years later Arthur Bentley, who worked for a while as a sociologist, published his classic study *Process of Government*, in which the idea of interest group has its origins (Bentley 1908).

In their discussions of interest all of these thinkers referred to what they saw as the deeply inspiring work of Gustav Ratzenhofer, especially *Die Sociologische Erkenntnis* (1898). Ratzenhofer was an officer in the Austrian army and the author of several works that proclaimed interest to be the basic force in nature as well as in society. According to Beat Huber in *Der Begriff des Interesses in den Sozialwissenschaften*, the first effort to develop a precise understanding of the concept of interest in the social sciences was undertaken precisely towards the end of the nineteenth century. She also notes that 'Ratzenhofer was the first author who made an attempt to systematically view social life from the perspective of interest' (Huber 1958: 6).

According to Ratzenhofer, there exists a basic force in the cosmos (*Urkraft*) which accounts for life and which also can be found among humans in the form of 'inborn interest' (Ratzenhofer 1898). What drives human behaviour, in other words, is interest. Sociology is defined by Ratzenhofer as the science of interaction or reciprocal influence (*Wechselbeziehungen*). Ratzenhofer, however, was also very careful to point out that sociology does not deal with an autonomous dimension of human life. The social behaviour of human beings depends not only on social interaction but also on other factors such as biology, psychology and so on. Similar to Comte, Ratzenhofer thought that sociology was a science whose main task was to synthesize the insights of the other sciences.

Besides presenting interest as a basic force, Ratzenhofer also supplied a typology of interests in his work. There are five types of interest: 'procreative interest', 'physiological interest', 'individual interest', 'social interest' and 'transcendental interest' (Ratzenhofer 1898: 54–66). Social interests are defined as interests that are related to consanguinity and group welfare. Each of the five types of interest produces 'impulses' towards action in human beings; and social life is what results when human beings act on these impulses. Social life, in other words, can only be understood if interests are taken into account; it has no inherent or independent dynamic. Ideas, for example, only become important in social life if they answer to people's needs or interests. 'It is the key of interests that unlocks the door of every treasure house of sociological lore', as Ratzenhofer once put it (Sorokin 1928: 643).

A common critique of Ratzenhofer is that his theory of interest is not so much sociological as psychological and/or biological. It is indeed true that his key work on interest, *Die Sociologische Erkenntnis*, can better be characterized as a philosophy-of-science type of work than as a study that elaborates on and specifies the role of interests in social life. None the less, Ratzenhofer did set interest on the agenda of sociology. And in doing so, he also pioneered what was to become a very popular strategy for how to introduce interest into sociological analysis, namely as a force that drives social relationships.

Ratzenhofer's American Followers (Albion Small, E.A. Ross and Arthur Bentley)

Ratzenhofer had a number of important followers, especially in the US, and Albion Small (1854–1926) was the foremost of these. Small took over many of Ratzenhofer's ideas about interest and also spread these very effectively, not least through *The American Journal of Sociology* in which he often published. Just as Ratzenhofer, he saw interest as part of nature; he also felt that it was necessary to develop a typology of interests; and he argued that interests constitute the master key to sociological analysis. 'Sociology', as Small put it in *General Sociology*, 'might be said to be the science of human interests and their workings under all conditions' (Small 1905: 442).

Like Ratzenhofer, Small saw interest as part of the cosmos: 'in the beginning were interests' (*ibid.*: 96). Just as the physicist makes the assumption that atoms constitute the basic units of matter, so the sociologist should make the assumption that interests constitute the basic units of human behaviour. 'The notion of interest is accordingly serving the same purpose in sociology which the notion of atoms has served in physical science' (*ibid.*: 426). No one has ever seen an atom, and it is the same with interests; they should be used because they are a useful abstraction.

According to Small, interests explain the force and strength with which people pursue certain goals in society. He describes, for example, in one place interest as a 'propulsion' and as 'an energetic pushing forward', and in another place as 'storage batteries of ... physical energy' (*ibid.*: 426–7). Small is also careful to draw a sharp conceptual line between interests as an object of study in biology and psychology, on the one hand, and in sociology on the other. While the former two sciences deal with interests as these are being constituted, sociology takes them for granted and begins with 'the finished product' (*ibid.*: 430).

According to Small, the centrality of interest to human action is absolute:

> Every act that every man performs is to be traced back to an interest. We eat because there is a desire for food; but the desire is set in motion by a bodily interest. We sleep because we are tired; but the weariness is a function of the bodily interest in re-building used-up tissue. We play because there is a bodily interest in the use of the muscles. We study because there is a mental interest in satisfying curiosity ... We go to the market to supply an economic interest, and to war because of some social interest of whatever mixed or simple form. (*ibid.*: 433)

Small, however, does not rest content with an undifferentiated concept of interest but argues that it is absolutely essential for modern sociology to develop a classification of interests. He suggests that there are six basic or elementary types of interest: health interest, wealth interest, sociability interest, knowledge interest, beauty interest and rightness interest. Each of these six interests can be subdivided further; and the health interest consists, for example, of the food interest, the sex interest and the work interest. All concrete actions by human beings, Small continues, are the products of these subdivided interests or of combinations of several interests: 'I have not been able to find any human act which requires, for explanation, any motive that cannot be accounted for by specialization and combination of these interests' (*ibid.*: 197).

In society interests either enter into conflict with one another or support one another. Small states that social processes typically contain a mixture of interests that conflict with one another or support one another. He also notes that it is common with conflicts in modern society; and it is clear that Small, like Ratzenhofer, belong to what is known in contemporary sociology as conflict theory. Small also emphasizes that existing social structures in society can either aid or block interest-driven actions. 'Institutions', we read, can operate as 'channels' for the actors as well as 'obstructions' (*ibid.*: 199).

While *General Sociology* contains many pages where the role of interests in social life is discussed on a very abstract level, little room is devoted to concrete examples. From one of the few examples that Small does provide, however, it is possible to get a sense of the value of his approach as an empirical tool. The example in question is how legislation against the use of alcohol has recently come about in some American states as well as the resistance that this type of legislation has encountered in these same states (*ibid.*: 438–9). While laws of this type and opposition to them may be seen as social facts in their own right, Small says, they are much better conceptualized in terms of interests: interests that support the law as well as interests that oppose it. It is only by outlining all of these interests, and laying bare their exact combination, that the sociologist will be in a position to understand fully what is going on.

Small suggests that six interests support the laws against the use of alcohol, while seven oppose it. Among the former are, for example, a 'moral interest' as well as 'a political interest in making capital out of a policy which would win certain voters'. Among the interests that oppose the laws are 'immoral interests' seeking gain at the expense of others; 'the interest in satisfying the drink appetite'; and 'the interest in personal freedom'. Small emphasizes that the interests that support the laws as well as those that are against them will vary in strength according to the concrete circumstances.

Small, in brief, continued the agenda of Ratzenhofer but also tried to improve upon it. Like Ratzenhofer, he attempted to account for the role of interest in different parts of society through the introduction of a typology. He, however, rejected the notion that interests are psychological or biological in nature through the argument that these two sciences deal with interest as they are being formed, while sociology only deals with interests once these have come into being. As opposed to Ratzenhofer, Small also explicitly asked the question how interests are related to the social structure. His answer was that these social structures can affect interests in two ways: either they operate as obstacles to the interests or as channels for them. Small, however, did not work these ideas out; they are just mentioned in a few lines in a book that is about 500 pages long. The end result, as in the case of Ratzenhofer, is a number of general statements about the importance of interests in society – but few concrete ideas about how one may introduce the idea of interests into sociological analysis in a meaningful manner.

Ratzenhofer had two important followers in the US besides Small. One of these was E.A. Ross (1866–1951) and the other Arthur Bentley (1870–1957). Ross's major work in which he advocated that sociology should be based on interests appeared in the very same year as Small's *General Sociology* and it was entitled *Foundations of Sociology* (1905). In it Ross outlined an approach to interests that is very similar to those of Ratzenhofer and Small. Interest is proclaimed to be the foundation of everything social; and a classification of interests is presented. According to Ross, there are four major types of interests and these 'constitute the chief history-making forces' (economic, political, religious and intellectual interests; Ross 1905: 170).

Even more fundamental than the interests, however, are what Ross calls 'desires', and there are nine different types of these ('appetitive', 'hedonic', 'egotic' and so on; *ibid.*: 169). While desires constitute 'the primary forces', interests are 'great complexes, woven of multicolored strands of desire, which shape society and make history' (*ibid.*: 168). Ross, in other words, suggests that impulses ('desires') drive interests, and not the other way around, as does Ratzenhofer.

Anyone who has studied the systems of Ratzenhofer and Small will find little that is new in Ross. On two points, however, Ross deserves some credit. First, he tried to associate the term 'social forces' with the concept of interests; and this was a happy choice since this expression nicely mixes a key feature of interest (its strength or force) with a terminology that has a genuine sociological touch to it (cf. MacIver 1932: 146). Secondly, Ross was among the first to try to theorize the concept of interest groups. *Social Foundations* contains, for example, a long section on this topic, even if the notion of interest group has mainly come to be associated with the work of Arthur Bentley.

The name of Arthur Bentley is today as forgotten in sociology as those of Ratzenhofer, Small and Ross. This is a pity because Bentley's study of interests, *The Process of Government* (1908), contains a number of sharp and useful ideas on interest and how it can be used in a sociological type of analysis. Take, for example, Bentley's skilful critique of Small and other thinkers who conceptualize interests as drives or impulses (Bentley 1908: 26–37). According to Bentley, this way of proceeding is inadmissible for two reasons. First, the assumption is made by Small that the individual has a number of interests *before* she enters society; and these interests are then used to explain what happens *in* society. Secondly, what Small actually does in his work, Bentley says, is to take various interests as these exist in society, project them onto the individual, and then use them to explain what happens in society. This type of reasoning 'reduces itself to the identical proposition A = A' (*ibid.*: 36–7).

Instead of proceeding in this manner, Bentley argues, one should start with the observation of what actually goes on in society and the many groups that make it up. If we do this, we realize that interests are the same as groups:

> There is no group without its interest. An interest, as the term will be used in this work, is the equivalent of a group. We may speak also of an interest group or of a group interest, again merely for the sake of clearness in expression. The group and the interest are not separate. There exists only one thing, that is, so many men bound together in or along the path of a certain activity. (*ibid.*: 211)

Bentley insists that interest is the same as group. He also equates interest with valuation; and his argument is that each group, as it acts, also expresses its valuation or interest. In order to understand what a group's interest consists of, strict empirical observation is necessary. It is inadmissible, for example, to proceed as economists do and assign some kind of objective value/interest to a group. 'If we should substitute for the actual interest of the activity some "objective utility", to use the economist's term, we should be going far astray, for no such "objective utility" appears ... at all' (*ibid.*: 213).

According to Bentley, groups are always defined in terms of other groups, and their interests are consequently also defined in terms of other interests. By this statement Bentley means as follows. A group of slaves is, for example, defined in relation to the group of slave owners as well as in relation to other groups in society. Similarly, the interests of, say, workers is defined by the group of employers and other groups in capitalist society.

To Bentley, in other words, the group is the basic unit of society, and therefore all you need to explain what happens. As part of this argument Bentley also rejects the notion that such factors as 'rules of the game' or tradition are useful as explanations (*ibid.*: 219, 318). Both of these, Bentley argues, are in reality nothing but the result of the activities or interests of groups. If we, for example, want to explain how groups evolve over time and through history, we are confronting a situation that is similar to explaining why an arrow follows a certain course. At each point of its course, Bentley argues, the flight of the arrow is the result of the forces that act on it; it is not the result of rules or tradition. In brief, interest is, as always, the key.

Interest and Social Forms (Georg Simmel)

Georg Simmel (1858–1918) is usually presented as a theoretician of modernity, sociability and intersecting social circles, so it may seem somewhat surprising to mention his name in a discussion of a 'realistic' concept such as interest. None the less, Simmel does discuss interest in his sociological work, including the key theoretical essay in *Soziologie*, which is called 'The Problem of Sociology'. In this and several other essays Simmel suggests a way of integrating interest into sociological theory that was quite popular at the time, namely as a force that led to the formation of social structure.

While Simmel once reviewed a book by Ratzenhofer on politics, it is currently not known if he also was familiar with what Ratzenhofer had written on interest (Frisby 2004). Still, it is clear that Simmel worked within the general approach to interest that is associated with the work of Ratzenhofer in the following sense. First, Simmel ascribed great importance to interests: they were truly *the* cause of human behaviour, including social behaviour. And secondly, Simmel saw interest as essentially an impulse or a drive that was pre-social.

From this point onwards, however, Simmel introduced a few small but crucial changes in his argument that make his approach quite different from that of Ratzenhofer. It should also be added that Simmel never engaged in the exercise of enumerating what interests exist, what they should be called, and how they should be ranked. As Simmel saw it, interests drive behaviour; and this behaviour will take different forms (and different names) once they become social. Interests, in other words, supply the force that drives the behaviour, which may take various social forms, such as subordination–superordination, competition, and so on. To cite the key formulation in 'The Problem of Sociology':

> Sociation is the form (realized in innumerably different ways) in which individuals grow together into a unity and within which their interests are realized. And it is on the basis of their interests – sensuous or ideal, momentary or lasting, conscious or unconscious, causal or teleological – that individuals form such unities. (Simmel [1908] 1971: 24)

A similar but considerably more engaging formulation of the same idea can be found in another Simmel classic, 'The Sociology of Sociability':

> On the one hand are the individuals in their directly perceptible existence, the bearers of the processes of association, who are united by these processes into the higher unity which one calls 'society'; on the other hand, the interests which, living in the individuals, motivate such union: economic and ideal interests, warlike and erotic, religious and charitable. To satisfy such urges and to attain such purposes, arise the innumerable forms of social life, all the one-with-another, for-one-another, in-one-another, against-one-another, and through-one-another, in state and commune, in church and economic associations, in family and clubs. The energy effects of atoms upon each other bring matter into the innumerable forms which we see as 'things'. Just so the impulses and interests, which a man experiences in himself and which push him out toward other men, bring about all the forms of association by which a mere sum of separate individuals are made into 'society'. (Simmel [1911] 1997: 120)

What Simmel says in this quotation sums up his position on the role of interest in society, except for one minor point. This is that just as one interest can take the expression of many different social forms, so different interests can take the expression of one and the same social form. Economic interests and sexual interests, for example, may both take the form of competition; and political interests and economic interests may be expressed in terms of, say, domination, conflict or subordination–superordination.

Simmel's position is thus the following: interests drive or propel human behaviour, and some of this behaviour is social in the sense that it deals with interaction. Social behaviour is understood by Simmel as taking different 'social forms'; and as examples of these forms Simmel mentions subordination–superordination, conflict, competition and so on. What distinguishes Simmel from Ratzenhofer, Small and Ross is, in other words, not very much, but still of some importance, namely that interests, once they have become part of the social world, take on an entirely new and social form. When they do this, they lose the name of 'interest' and are from now on exclusively referred to as sociological terms. Interest, in other words, disappears but still operates as the invisible cause of what happens in society.

Interest as Foundation for a Sociological Theory (James Coleman)

While the distance in years between Simmel and James Coleman (1926–1995) is large – more than half a century – there are, none the less, some distinct parallels between the way they approach interest and its role in sociological explanation. Both, for example, attach a very important role to it; interest is essentially what drives social action. Both also preferred to translate interest into social terms rather than use it as a sociological concept in its own right.

Coleman was not influenced by Simmel's ideas on interest or at least he does not refer to these. He was, on the other hand, familiar with the broad outlines of the history of the concept of interest, primarily through the writings of Albert O. Hirschman (1977, 1986). Beyond this, we know that Coleman had studied the ideas of Arthur Bentley; he was also deeply knowledgeable in economics.

Coleman began to experiment with the idea that interest should be central to sociological analysis some time in the 1960s (Coleman 1986: 15), and he was still fascinated by this idea at the time of his death in 1995. The place where he made his most sustained attempt to develop a way to integrate the concept of interest into sociological analysis is in *Foundations of Social Theory* (1990). The core theoretical ideas in this work are to be found in Chapter 2 ('Actors and Resources, Control and Interest'), which means that they come after the famous analysis of the micro–macro problem in Chapter 1. If the fact that Coleman chose *not* to present his discussion of interest in the first chapter is the reason why his ideas on this topic have not been much discussed by sociologists, is difficult to know. They are in any case important, not least because Coleman did propose a novel and original way of introducing the concept of interest into sociology.

In Chapter 2 of *Foundations of Social Theory* Coleman cites

Hélvetius's statement that interest should hold the same position in the analysis of the moral (or social) universe as the laws of movement in the analysis of the physical world, and adds that this position is 'close' to his own (*ibid.*: 28). That interest constitutes the very foundation of Coleman's theory of social action becomes abundantly clear when he also states that the sociologist should start with the idea of interest, more precisely with the notion that the actor always attempts to maximize her self-interest, and go from there. Coleman's reference to maximization of self-interest shows the influence on his thought by economics. Coleman, however, does not want to turn sociology into economics but rather improve sociology by introducing some ideas from economics into it. Just as Coleman advocated the introduction of social structure into economic analysis (to cite the title of one of his articles), one can say that he wanted to introduce interests into sociological analysis (Coleman 1984).

The way that Coleman goes about this project in Chapter 2 in *Foundations* is as follows. An actor is assumed to have an interest in an object or event, but in order to satisfy this interest she also has to have 'control' over 'the resources' that are of interest to her. If the actor does have control over the resources in which she is interested, there will be no social action. If, however, we turn to the situation in which two actors have an interest in the resources that the other actor controls, then the two actors will interact with one another, and we have what Coleman terms a social system. Coleman illustrates his argument with a simple figure (see Figure 3.1).

Figure 3.1 Coleman's model of how interests drive social action

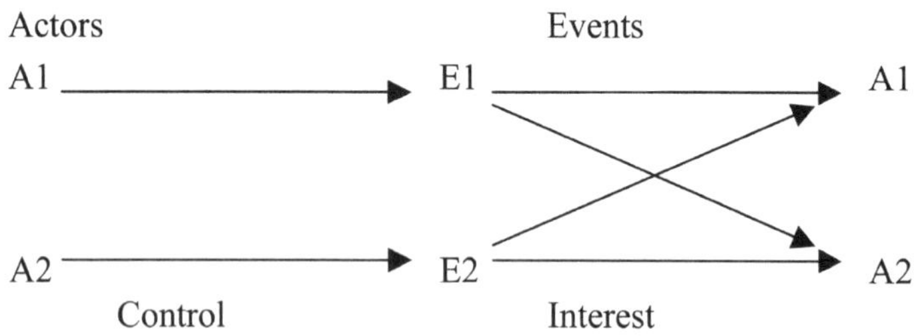

Note: Coleman presents this figure of how interests drive social interaction in Chapter 2 in *Foundations of Social Theory*. The main novelty in this scheme is the idea that in order for an actor to satisfy her interest, she needs control over the resources that are of interest to her.

While Coleman makes the same move as Simmel in his argument that interest drives action, and that this action has to be social if the interest is to be satisfied, there also exist important differences between their arguments. For one thing, Coleman introduces two new concepts to better handle the notion of interest: 'control' and 'resources'. Coleman also rejects the idea that interest is something pre-social/psychological and, in so doing, follows the lead of the economists. As to the existence of norms, Coleman states that these undoubtedly play a central role in society but that it is imperative to break with the sociologists' tendency to take these for granted and not present an argument as to why they exist in the first place. One way to do so, according to Coleman, would be to start with interests and go from there. Norms, in short, can and should be related to actions driven by interests.

Coleman's way of formulating his ideas in Chapter 2 of *Foundations* shows that he wanted to develop a sociology based on interest, and that the way to do this was to add the ideas of control and resources. This, however, is not how he proceeds in *Foundations*, and while the rest of this work indeed testifies to the author's attempt to assign a central role to interest in sociology, this is instead done in an *ad hoc* manner that has little to do with control and resources. Social capital, for example, is defined as social relations of the kind that are needed to realize an interest (*ibid.*: 305). Coleman's analysis of the labour market and the firm draw primarily on agency theory, which, according to Coleman, is essentially sociological since it is based on the interaction between the agent, the principal and a third party (*ibid.*: 152). Weber's analysis of bureaucracy is criticized on the ground that workers are not simply following orders and behaving like bureaucrats; they also have their own distinct interests. Norms, finally, come into being, according to Coleman, as part of a conscious effort by an actor to realize her interest (*ibid.*: 242, 422).

While it again deserves to be pointed out that Coleman presents his own theory about how to introduce interest into sociology in Chapter 2 of *Foundations*, but fails to apply it in much of the book, he should, none the less, be credited with having made an important attempt to take the concept of interest and give it a sociological twist in the analysis of a series of important topics. Beyond the ones that have just been alluded to, a special mention should also be made of his discussion of corporate actors and their interests. While earlier sociologists usually only assigned interest to single individuals or aggregates of individuals, Coleman was fascinated by the idea of a fictitious actor that came into being in the Middle Ages and in the nineteenth century led to the notion of the corporation as a legal personality. According to Coleman, the idea of the modern corporation constituted an exceptionally important social invention.

Approach 2: Interest as a Major Force in Social Life

All the sociologists who have just been discussed, from Ratzenhofer to Coleman, have in common that they regard interest as *the* major force or *Urkraft* in social life; interest accounts for most of what is going on. This idea is worked out in different ways; and while Bentley, for example, views social life as totally dominated by group interests, Simmel sees it as exclusively consisting of social forms, all of which are driven by interests. Some of the thinkers work with interests in their pre-social forms, be they biological or psychological (Ratzenhofer, Small, Ross), while others see them as social or as an assumption along the lines of economists (Bentley, Coleman).

The sociologists who will be discussed in this section differ from Ratzenhofer *et al.* in that they view interest as an important force in social life, but also that they try to delimit and specify the role of interest. In doing so, as we soon shall see, they follow different strategies. Max Weber attempts to pinpoint the areas of social life where interest, and primarily economic interest, plays a key role. Pierre Bourdieu, in contrast, makes interest into a part of his general theory of sociology. Both Weber's and Bourdieu's attempts can be described as sustained, even though none of them paid any attention whatsoever to the history of interest or earlier attempts to use it for sociological purposes.

Weber uses the term 'interest' very often; in many different places in his work; and also in many different meanings. A frequency count shows that *Interesse* and related terms come after *Sinn* (meaning) and related concepts (3,426) with 2,786 hits, but before, say, *Handeln* (action) (1,511), *Kultur* (culture) (1,207) and words related to *Soziologie* (602; Weber 1999). In this chapter I will primarily focus on Weber's use of interest in *Economy and Society* since this is the place where one can find his most concentrated attempt to introduce interest into his sociological categories. After having presented Weber's ideas on how interest can be used in sociology – essentially by being integrated (Weber suggests) in various sociological concepts – I will also comment on his famous statement (in another work) that material and ideal interest drive human behaviour, and that ideas sometimes can operate as switchmen for interest-driven action.

Economy and Society 1: Regular Behaviour that is Interest-driven

The term *Interesse* does not appear in the crucial first paragraph in Chapter 1 in *Economy and Society*, in which Weber presents his general sociology, nor in the equally important twenty pages of explication that is appended to it. The term 'interest' does, however, play a prominent role in one of the first paragraphs in Chapter 1, namely in paragraph 4, entitled 'Types of Action Orientation: Usage, Custom, Self-Interest'.

According to this paragraph, there are certain empirical uniformities or regularities in social life that are of much interest to the sociologist, since they involve distinct types of behaviour. Three such types are *usage* (or regular social action), *custom* (or social action that is of long standing), and social action that is 'determined by self-interest' ('*bedingt durch Interessenlage* ["*Interessenbedingt*"]'). The latter type of regularity is described as follows: 'a uniformity of orientations . . . if and insofar as the actors' conduct is instrumentally (*zweckrational*) oriented toward identical expectations' (Weber [1922] 1978: 29).

What is important about this statement is first of all Weber's description of interest-driven action as essentially 'instrumental' (*zweckrational*). By using this term Weber connects interest-driven action to the typology of social action that is presented in paragraph 2 ('Types of Social Action'). Interest-driven action should therefore be understood as being the collective version of instrumental action. In its capacity as instrumental action it also consists essentially of two parts: (1) 'the actor's own rationally pursued and calculated ends'; and (2) that other actors (as well as objects) are taken into account (Weber [1922] 1978: 24). To this should be added that instrumental rational action in principle is action that it is carried out with a high degree of consciousness, and that it stands in contrast to 'traditional social action' and 'affectual social action' in this respect. The reader may recall that value-rational action, in contrast, is characterized by the fact that the actor is exclusively driven by values that are consciously taken into account, and that it is pursued without regard to success.

In his explication of the paragraph on social action, Weber uses the market to illustrate regular behaviour that is interest-driven as well as collective. If a market actor is (instrumentally) rational, she will orient her behaviour in an impersonal way to other market actors, in order to realize her economic interest. The more that this is done – that is, the more the behaviour is oriented to what Weber in paragraph 4 calls 'identical expectations' – the more the behaviour in the market will be rational and interest driven. Weber also points out that actors who deviate from this behaviour will hurt themselves; they will also create difficulties for the other actors and thereby evoke their anger.

Weber also points to some interesting qualities of so-called interest-driven behaviour. For one thing, this type of behaviour, according to Weber, is often much sturdier than behaviour that is just oriented to norms. Or, as he puts it, uniformities of this type 'are far more stable than they would be if actions were oriented to a system of norms and duties which were considered binding on the members of the group' (*ibid.*: 30).

Secondly, Weber notes that economists have been very interested in the fact that there are interest-driven regularities of great stability. Indeed, this has been one of the circumstances, Weber says, that has made 'economics [possible] as a science' (*ibid.*). Marginal utility economics from the early twentieth century was, of course, based on the notion of interest-driven behaviour – but has nothing to say about norm-driven or customary behaviour.

Thirdly, Weber adds that interest-driven regular behaviour, which figures so prominently in the economic sphere, can also be found 'in all other spheres of action as well' (*ibid.*). This is important since it means that interest-driven behaviour can be found not only in the sphere of the economy, but also in those of politics, religion, intellectual life and erotic life. Weber writes: 'This type, with its distinct awareness and lack of feeling bound, is the polar antithesis of every sort of unthinking acquiescence in customary ways as well as of devotion to norms consciously accepted as absolute values' (*ibid.*; my translation). Two things, then, primarily characterize interest-driven behaviour: '*distinct awareness*' and '*lack of feeling bound*'.

Fourthly, Weber suggests that interest-driven behaviour of the regular kind becomes more common as the world becomes more rational. This point is reminiscent of Tocqueville's argument that interest is central to democracies but not to aristocracies. Customs recede, Weber continues, and are replaced by market-oriented and similar types of behaviour. Or in Weber's words: 'One of the most important aspects of the process of "rationalization" of action is the substitution for the unthinking acceptance of ancient custom, of deliberate adaptation to situations in terms of self-interest' (*ibid.*). Weber ends his discussion of interest-driven regular behaviour by saying that the 'process of rationalization' does not necessarily have to consist of instrumentally rational behaviour, of the type that is discussed in paragraph 4; it can also be value-rational. This is a very important addition, to which I shall return later in this book.

Lastly, immediately following paragraph 4 Weber makes the point that for an order to be stable, it cannot exclusively rest on interest (or violence); it also has to be perceived as valid or binding (*ibid.*: 31–8). This legitimacy, as Weber terms it, comes about through norms and is sometimes also enforced through law. Given the prevalence of legitimate orders in most societies, it seems clear that, for Weber, interests are typically closely associated with norms.

Economy and Society 2: The Role of Interests in Associative Relationships or Associations

As Chapter 1 in *Economy and Society* progresses, the social phenomena that are discussed become increasingly complex; and Weber advances from social action, to social relationship, to organizations, and so on. This is also true for social phenomena that have something to do with interests, as exemplified by the advance from paragraph 4 on 'Types of Action Orientation' to paragraph 9 on 'Communal and Associative Relationships' (*ibid.*: 40–3). While a communal relationship, according to *Economy and Society*, is characterized by a sense among the actors that they all belong together, an associative relationship is characterized by the fact that it rests on interests that are rationally adjusted to one another or balanced against each other (*Vergemeinschaftung* versus *Vergesellschaftung*).

Associative relationships or associations, Weber states, can be found in their purest version in the following three forms: (1) market exchange (where compromises between opposed interests are common); (2) instrumental associations based on the material interests of the members (*Zweckverein*); and (3) associations devoted to a cause and of a value-rational nature (*Gesinnungsverein*). A modern corporation would be an example of an instrumental and interest-based association, and so would what Weber elsewhere in *Economy and Society* terms interest groups (*Interessenverbände*; *ibid.*: 297–9). A religious sect, on the other hand, would be an example of a value-rational association.

Weber emphasizes that associative relationships or associations are conflictual in nature, in that they are based on interests that oppose each other. This means that there will either be compromises (as in the market) or a continuous opposition of interests (as in an instrumental association). Weber also points out that most relationships or associations are communal in nature to some extent, including those that at first may seem to be exclusively motivated by rationally pursued economic interests. 'Any social relationship' that 'lasts for long periods', Weber emphasizes, will have elements of communal feelings, including relationships in work places and offices (*ibid.*: 41). The conflicts, however, will be played out within the relationship or association.

Weber mentions rational market transactions as an example of associative relationships or associations, and this reminds us of his earlier discussion in paragraph 4 of interest-driven regularities. Little that is new appears, however, to be added to this type of phenomenon in paragraph 9, except that Weber here focuses on the *interaction* between two market actors which is typically brief.

But Weber also expands his use of the concept of interest in paragraph 9 in an important way. He does this when it comes to rational and interest-driven actions that form into something of a permanent nature that Weber terms a *Verein* and which may simply be translated as an organization. These organizations can be value-rational, as sects tend to be, or instrumentally rational, as firms tend to be; and it seems clear that the latter are far more common and also far more important in contemporary society.

Weber's terminology when it comes to organizations is notoriously complex, and at this point it deserves to be pointed out that political organizations may also be formed in order to further ordinary interests, including of course the state. Weber draws a sharp conceptual distinction between relationships that are inspired by economic interests and are (formally) *voluntary*, on the one hand, and relationships that are the result of domination, power and violence, and are ruled by *authority*, on the other. But this, to repeat, should not distract us from realizing that not only economic organizations but also many other types of organizations are based on interests, and – more generally – from arriving at the conclusion that interest-driven behaviour is central to most organizations in modern society.

Economy and Society 3: Interest in the Concepts of Class and Status

Weber also suggests that the concept of interest can play an important role in another sociological category, namely that of *class*. Weber's theoretical writings on class are primarily to be found in Chapter 4 in *Economy and Society* and in a chapter in the 'old' part of this work, that is, in the part that was to be discarded after it had been rewritten and slimmed down (*ibid.*: 302–7, 926–39). Since Weber died before he could carry out his plans in this respect, however, both the section that he rewrote for Chapter 4, and the old version, were included in what we today know as *Economy and Society*.

While the concept of interest is present in the discussion of class in Chapter 4, it is much more frequently used (and also easier to study) in the discussion of class in the 'old' chapter in *Economy and Society*; and I will therefore primarily refer to the latter text. That Weber did not use the concept of interest very much in Chapter 4 should not be understood to mean that he had now come to think that it was not as helpful as he had once thought. Its absence is more likely due to the fact that although Weber often used the idea of interest, he did not necessarily always use this word.

According to Weber, the modern concept of class rests exclusively on economic interest. 'The factor that creates "class" ', we read in *Economy and Society*, 'is unambiguously economic interest, and indeed, only interests involved in the existence of the market' (*ibid.*: 928). As opposed to Marx, however, Weber sees class more as a factor that decides the socio-economic fate of the individual than as a collective actor of its own. What class an individual belongs to in a market economy will decide his or her 'life chances', as Weber famously phrased it.

Weber also discusses Marx's concept of class interest; and his basic stance is that this concept becomes 'ambiguous' as soon as you go beyond the general statement that a huge number of people who share the same economic interests are likely to behave in a similar way (*ibid.*: 928–29). On the other hand, there do exist several factors that may channel interest-driven behaviour of the individual member of a class in different 'directions' (*Richtungen*; *ibid.*: 929). One of these is the skill of the individual worker: whether he or she has a lot of talent for the task in question, just average talent, or no talent at all (*ibid.*). Another factor that may determine the 'direction' of the interest-driven action has to do with the extent to which collective social action is available to the actor – whether it is to some extent, or to a large extent, and also if organizations such as trade unions are present.

Before leaving the discussion of interest and Weber's concept of class, it should be noted that Weber famously contrasts the concept of class to that of status. While the former is decided by economic interest and production, the latter has to do with honour, lifestyle and consumption. Just as there is 'class society', there also is 'status society' (*ibid.*: 306). If we look at the important Chapter 4, titled 'Status Groups and Classes', however, we also note that Weber only uses the concept of interest in his discussion of class, not in his discussion of status. But this must by no means be seen as a sign that interests are somehow less important in a status society than in a class society. It is perfectly clear from Weber's analysis elsewhere in *Economy and Society* that people fight just as hard for their interests in a status society as in a class society. Weber also uses the expression 'status interests' (*ständische Interessen*) at one point in his work (e.g. Weber 1991: 16). We are again encountering a case, in other words, in which Weber uses other words for interest, and where the absence of the term 'interest' should not be read as the absence of the idea of interest.

In the next section we shall turn to Weber's famous discussion of 'material and ideal interests', and a status society can perhaps best be described as a type of society that rests on a different combination of interests than a class society. As opposed to a class society, the economic interests in a status society are not centred around the market, but around the processes of redistribution and reciprocity. Ideal interests also play much more of a role in a status society since honour and lifestyle are central.

Ideas as Switchmen for Interest-driven Action

When Weber in 1919–1920 revised the text that was to serve as the introduction to *The Economic Ethics of the World Religions*, he added the following passage, which has become classic:

> Not ideas, but material and ideal interests (*Interessen*), directly govern men's conduct. Yet very frequently the 'world images' that have been created by 'ideas' have, like switchmen, determined the tracks along which action has been pushed by the dynamic of interest. (Weber [1920] 1946: 280)

This passage is among the most cited and discussed in the secondary literature on Weber, and it raises a topic that has not yet been discussed, namely the relationship of interests to ideas. Its main emphasis is on what we may call the double relationship of ideas to interests. Ideas are, first of all, *not* what primarily drives or motivates human beings – interests are. Secondly, *some* ideas may orient people's actions in different directions. Weber's metaphor can be rewritten as follows: human actions are propelled forward by interests, like a train at full speed – but in a direction that the switchmen decide.

Weber's quote on the switchmen is also important for its formulation of 'ideal and material interests'. This is a happy formulation in that it draws attention to the fact that there exists no inherent contradiction between ideals and (economic) interests; both can operate as powerful forces on human behaviour. It would also seem clear that in some cases ideal interests – as expressed in, say, certain types of political or religious actions – can be much stronger than economic interests. It is easy enough to find occasions in history when people have chosen to die for their religious or political ideals, but no one has yet heard of economic martyrs.

While the quote about the switchmen is often discussed in the secondary literature on Weber, and while the expression 'material and ideal interests' is often commented on in this type of work, there is little discussion of the fact that Weber also uses this expression in many other parts of his work. One of Weber's earliest insights as a researcher was that even though it was in the economic interest of poor agricultural workers to remain on the huge landed estates in Germany, east of the river Elbe, they preferred, none the less, to migrate to the cities where the economic prospects were considerably worse. What drove them to go counter to their economic interest, Weber says, was 'the *magic* of freedom' (Weber 1994: 8).

In quite a few places in *Economy and Society* Weber also uses the exact expression 'material and ideal interests' or expressions that are very close to it (for the exact expression, see e.g. Weber [1922] 1978: 246 [twice], 315, 287, 1129; for expressions that are very close, see e.g. Weber [1922] 1978: 202, 224, 264). In all of these places Weber appears to regard these two types of interest as summarizing the main forces that drive human behaviour. They are not, however, the only forces that do so, as the famous switchmen quotation reminds us; ideas (here in the form of religion) must also be taken into account.

What this leaves us with is that Weber seems to suggest that the concept of interest can be used in sociology in two different ways. On the one hand, it can be used to construct specific sociological concepts, such as 'class' and 'associative relationships'. On the other hand, it can also be used as a short-hand to indicate the main forces that drive people's behaviour. While the second use is typically open to the charge of tautology, Weber avoids this to some extent by assigning a decisive role to other factors, summarized as 'ideas' and which perhaps not only cover religion but also other ways of viewing the world. Weber's 'ideas' not only have the power to steer behaviour in different directions; they can also at certain junctures make human behaviour *change* direction.

Bourdieu

The second major sociologist who has been an advocate of using the concept of interest in a precise and delimited way is Pierre Bourdieu. There exists a link between Weber's use of the concept of interest and that of Bourdieu. More precisely, Bourdieu studied Weber's sociology of religion early on and was especially influenced by his analysis of religious interests (Bourdieu [1971] 1987). Weber's way of handling interest, as Bourdieu saw it, represented a very effective way to counter idealism in sociology as well as the attempt to explain social facts with the help of psychological concepts such as motive and impulse.

Bourdieu's main writings on interest consist of two brief articles, 'The Interest of the Sociologist' and 'Is a Disinterested Act Possible?' (Bourdieu [1981] 1990, [1988] 1998). Especially the latter is rich and original, very similar in argument but also sharper in its formulations than the section on interest in the popular introduction to Bourdieu's ideas, *An Invitation to Reflexive Sociology* (Bourdieu and Wacquant 1992: 115–20). For Bourdieu's ideas on religious interest and his link to Weber, the reader is especially referred to 'Legitimation and Structured Interests in Weber's Sociology of Religion' (Bourdieu [1971] 1987).

The concept of interest always appears in Bourdieu's sociology in close connection with a discussion of habitus and the field. Together these three concepts, plus the notion of different capitals, constitute the core of Bourdieu's sociology and the grid that he applies to all topics. The key idea is that certain areas of society constitute a distinct social space with their own fundamental laws; that the actors in these fields all have a distinct disposition or habitus, based on earlier experience; and that they only participate in a field if they have an interest in it. Each field has its own distinct interest; and there are consequently as many interests as there are fields. As examples of fields, Bourdieu mentions religion, the economy and the literary world. Similarly there are religious interests, economic interests, literary interests, and so on.

Bourdieu is careful to distinguish the way in which he himself uses the concept of interest from the way that it is used in economics. The way that the economists handle interest, he warns, entails 'the degree zero of sociology'; he also refers to *homo economicus* as a kind of 'anthropological monstrosity' (Bourdieu 1993: 77, 2005: 82). There are several reasons why the economists' use of the concept should be avoided, according to Bourdieu. For one, economists only see one type of interest, while in reality there are many. The tendency of economists to apply their own model of economic interest to all other areas of society, Bourdieu terms 'economism' (Bourdieu [1988] 1998: 83). Economists, finally, are wrong in making the assumption that actors focus on their interests in a deliberate manner, decide how to realize them, and then do so. The way Bourdieu sees it, is that people approach reality through their habitus, which means that they approach it in an instinctive rather than in a conscious manner. People, Bourdieu says, act in a reasonable manner, not in a rational manner.

Bourdieu's definition of interest is original and differs not only from the way that other sociologists have conceptualized it but also from earlier thinkers. Interest, Bourdieu suggests, is close to the terms *illusio, investment* and *libido*. A field can be described as a 'social game', and only those actors who become drawn into the game and want to be part of it will display an interest in it. The opposite of interest is indifference or what Bourdieu, with the Stoics, terms *ataraxia*. In this case you do not see the point of the game; it simply leaves you cold.

As is clear from what has just been said, the main thrust of Bourdieu's thought is that interests constitute social constructions. 'Anthropology and comparative history show that the properly social magic of institutions can constitute just about anything as an interest' (Bourdieu and Wacquant 1992: 117). Whether Bourdieu's stance also means that *all* interests are social constructions and nothing else is not equally clear. At one point in his discussion of interest Bourdieu says that 'biological libido' can be characterized as 'an undifferentiated impulse' and always turns into 'social libido', and at another that it only makes sense to use the term 'religious need' if the need is particularized and anchored in social relations (Bourdieu [1971] 1987: 122, [1988] 1998: 78).

Another creative contribution by Bourdieu to the sociological analysis of interest has to do with his ideas about disinterestedness. According to Bourdieu, being disinterested is not the same as being indifferent to a game. Being disinterested means that you do have an investment in the social game but that this investment makes you *appear* indifferent to those who are outside the field. A religious person may show utter indifference to money, just as a nobleman or an artist does. What matters to the believer is her relationship to God; to the nobleman, honour; and to the artist, art.

According to Bourdieu, however, showing disinterest by the believer and so on is in reality simply how you have to behave when you pursue an interest in the specific field you are in. Bourdieu writes in 'Is There A Disinterested Act?':

> At the beginning of *The Court Society*, Norbert Elias cites the example of a duke who gives a purse full of crowns to his son. When he questions him six months later and the son boasts of not having spent the money, the duke takes the purse and throws it out the window. He thus gives his son a lesson of disinterestedness, gratuitousness, and nobility; but it is also a lesson of investment of symbolic capital, which suits the aristocratic universe. (Bourdieu [1988] 1998: 86)

Approach 3: Interest as Being of Little or No Importance

While it is rare to find direct attacks on the concept of interest in sociological works, this concept is, none the less, often *de facto* missing from the analysis and by implication regarded as of little or no importance. Part of this neglect probably has to do with the strength of economics and the tendency in this discipline to equate interest exclusively with economic self-interest. Sociologists, by tradition, do not like greed and economists. There is also a distinct tendency in modern sociology to see itself as capable of explaining everything that goes on in society through concepts such as social relations, social structure, networks and so on – that is, without referring to interests. One example of this is so-called relational sociology but there are others as well (e.g. Emirbayer 1997).

One of the best-known attacks on the concept of interest in modern sociology can be found in the work of Talcott Parsons, especially in *The Structure of Social Action* (1937). The main argument in this famous work is that sociology has been increasingly successful in breaking with the utilitarian tradition of seeing interests as the key to social science analysis, and that this is a development that is extremely important and must be continued. Parsons states that Hobbes realized that if everybody followed their self-interest, there would be a war of all against all; and that this is the reason why there has to be a sovereign.

Many other thinkers, however, have instead followed a practice initiated by Locke, according to Parsons, which is to assume that people will realize on their own why they must not fight with one another, and that this is the reason why there is no war of all against all. This type of solution to the problem of order depends, again according to Parsons, on the assumption of a 'natural identity of interests' (Parsons [1937] 1968: 96–7). What Locke's solution misses, however, is the one element that is imperative to ensure order in society, and this is *norms*. According to Parsons, norms constitute 'the ultimate source of power', while interest is 'a brittle thing' (Parsons [1937] 1968: 404).

A similar hostility to the notion of interest can be found in the work of John Meyer, who is a major figure in contemporary sociology. In a well-known article entitled 'Institutionalized Organizations: Formal Structure as Myth and Ceremony', one can find an argument that is centred around a very special view of interests (Meyer and Rowan 1977). Modern organizations, it is here suggested, exist in a world in which there is a very high premium on taking interests into account in a rational manner; and if this is not done, the survival of the organization will be in jeopardy. This ideology of interest and rationality, however, is so out of touch with reality that the only way for an organization to survive, if it adopts it, is to decouple its formal structure from its everyday practices. Organizations, in short, must appear to do one thing (be 'rational') but in reality do something else.

It has been pointed out by Paul DiMaggio that Meyer and his school primarily focus on 'interest-free models and explanations', and that this may have its origin in Meyer's attempt to respond to the strong revival of utilitarianism that followed on the decline of Parsonianism (DiMaggio 1988: 4). What is positive about Meyer's project, DiMaggio continues, is that it has succeeded in locating and drawing attention to precisely those factors that prevent people from recognizing their interests. But DiMaggio also argues that if one proceeds in this way, there is only a limited number of topics to which Meyer's type of analysis can be applied. Precisely for this reason new institutionalism (as this approach is called) should pay more attention to topics such as agency as well as interest.

In his more recent work, however, Meyer has chosen to do exactly the opposite of what DiMaggio recommends, with the result that interest has totally vanished from his analysis. Meyer's argument today is that the concept of interest as well as that of the individual are not very helpful in social science analysis; indeed, they obstruct it. In order to get at the core of things, Meyer argues, it is imperative to go beyond these two categories and realize that they are part of a very special type of Western culture, namely the liberalism of Anglo-American origins that has become popular after World War II. 'The liberal model legitimates an actor (a self or an interest) as an abstract, rather contentless, entity in space' (Meyer and Jepperson 2000: 109). Meyer also says that making the assumption that there are individual actors with distinct interests turns these into 'small gods' in the analysis (Meyer 2000: 239).

Concluding Remarks

The account in this chapter of the works of Ratzenhofer and others shows that there has been little continuity over time in the sociological literature when it comes to interest, in the sense that sociologists have not been aware of the way in which other sociologists have used this concept. This represents a problem in its own right; it also constitutes a reason for grouping the various sociologists into the three categories of this chapter and going through their arguments in detail.

The first strategy – to see interest as *the* major force in social life – can be faulted on the ground of tautology, since there are no other factors that drive behaviour. Or to phrase it differently: by assuming that everything that happens is the result of one or several interests you simply recast the whole thing in terms of interests. One is reminded of the famous line in one of Molière's comedies in which a doctor explains that opium puts people to sleep because it has 'sleep-inducing powers (*virtus dormitiva*)' (Molière [1673] 1907: 328).

Several of the sociologists who have been in favour of seeing interest as *the* major cause of what happens in social life have also failed to draw a proper line between the realms of biology and psychology, on the one hand, and that of the social, on the other. Ratzenhofer, Small and Ross are all guilty on this count. One of the important drawbacks of this approach is that it easily leads to a position where one and the same cause (in the psychological–biological realm) is used to account for a number of different phenomena (in the social realm).

None the less, the advocates of seeing interest as the major force in social life have also produced some fruitful ideas which deserve to be part of the discussion. For one thing, Ross tried to associate the concept of interest with that of 'social forces', which is good idea since interest implies power and strength on a collective level. Simmel, in contrast, suggested that all social forms that exist were the result of interests – but in the process eliminated all references to the force or strength that characterize interest-driven social behaviour. Finally, while the writings of Ratzenhofer, Small and Ross may seem dated today, it is different with the works of Bentley and Coleman which are still sharp and worth reading.

The second strategy – to assign a major role to interest in the sociological explanation, but together with other factors – avoids the danger of tautology. That it is also possible to treat interest as one among several factors in very different ways was illustrated by the work of Weber and Bourdieu. Weber's main strategy was to centre sociological concepts directly around interest (e.g. 'uniform behaviour determined by self-interest') or let it be an integral part of them (e.g. 'class' and 'associative relationships'). By proceeding in this manner, Weber succeeded in creating several useful sociological concepts. Still, Weber's treatment of interest is not wholly satisfactory. He, for example, does not explain what he means by interest and proceeds as if its meaning is obvious. Weber also uses this concept in very different ways – as one of several factors in middle-range concepts, but also as *the* major driving forces in society, as in the famous line about 'material and ideal interests'.

Bourdieu's way of handling interest is quite different from that of Weber, in the sense that he makes it an organic part of his own general theory of sociology. Bourdieu, in other words, positions the concept of interest at a level where it can only be used by sociologists who also accept his ideas about field, habitus and so on. Furthermore, while the idea that every field has its own interest may at first seem useful, there is little theoretical discussion in Bourdieu's work about what happens when the interests of all fields collide.

As opposed to Weber, however, Bourdieu does provide an explanation of what interest is, and he does this in an imaginative and original way. Bourdieu also spells out explicitly an idea that is only implicit in Weber, namely that interests should be conceptualized as social constructions. The links of interest to the biological and psychological realms are, in other words, severed in Bourdieu's work, and the scene is set for a purely sociological analysis of interest along the lines of Durkheim's dictum that only social facts should be used to explain other social facts.

Finally, the third strategy – to view interests as being of little or no importance – risks reducing everything that happens in social life to culture, values, norms and the like. It is probably no accident that Talcott Parsons and John Meyer, who are both social systems thinkers and reject methodological individualism, are hostile to using the notion of interest in sociological explanations; and the reason for this is as follows. Thinkers who start with the individual must face the problem of explaining how an individual can survive, and this usually leads to a discussion of work, interest or the like. Systems theoreticians and holists, in contrast, do not find it equally urgent to address this question since a system is an abstract entity and easily lends itself to an analysis exclusively in terms of symbols, culture and the like.

It should also be noted that both Parsons and Meyer are somewhat ambivalent in their attitude to interest in that they simultaneously appear to reject it and approve of it. Parsons, for example, praises Weber for his use of the concept of religious interest in *The Structure of Social Action* but also criticizes the general concept of interest in the same work; and Meyer argues that the formal organization is often a 'rational myth', while he simultaneously says that it is 'efficiency criteria' (read: interest) that drive the informal organization. The key to their ambivalence may be that they follow the economists in equating interest with economic interest.

While the sociologists discussed in this chapter have proposed several different ways in which the concept of interest can be incorporated into sociological analysis, they have by no means solved all the problems involved in this enterprise. Neither have they succeeded in establishing interest as a standard sociological concept. What would a modern definition of interest look like? How can it be used in empirical research and be operationalized? And how is it related to, say, the concept of institution? These are some of the questions that will be discussed in the next chapter.

4

Interest as Activity and Analogy

This chapter is centred around two topics. First, I will present some ideas on interest that have not yet been mentioned but which should be part of the discussion for this to be reasonably complete. And second, I will suggest a new way in which to approach the concept of interest: what we mean by this term and how it may be used in social science analysis.

As to the first task, it is clear that something has to be said about the way that the concept of interest has been used in modern economics as well as in political science. In all brevity, interest has continued to be very important to economics, and some new and suggestive uses have also been found for it. In political science the notion of interest group has become a standard concept; and interest has also found its way into modern political science in some other ways as well.

Why a new approach to interest is needed, and what can be accomplished through such an approach, will be addressed in the latter half of this chapter. I will argue that interest should continue to be a key concept in social science but also that current attempts to conceptualize it are unsatisfactory for a number of reasons. In short, something needs to be done to move the discussion of interest from its current level to a new level. I will attempt to do so, and I will also give several examples of how interest can be used to address important problems in social science. The ones I have chosen are: how objectivity can be ensured; what the structure of institutions looks like; and what can turn ideas into powerful social forces.

The Role of Interest in Modern Economics

During the course of the twentieth century economics has become a highly successful social science, inside academia as well as in the eyes of the public and those with power in society. This has had several consequences for the predominant way in which the concept of interest is understood, again within academia as well as outside it. What has happened in all brevity is that interest is primarily seen as having only one meaning today, and that is as economic interest in the sense of economic self-interest. 'Mainstream economic theory has solidified around the assumption of simple pursuit of self-interest', to cite a recent work by Amartya Sen (1997: xv). This whole development, as already mentioned, has also put an end to the much more flexible and broader concept of interest that was in use during earlier centuries.

But there is also the fact that modern economics has spearheaded a number of new and important uses of the concept of interest, which all rest on the notion that the actor is exclusively driven by economic interest. A few of these will be discussed in this chapter – such as the theory of revealed preference, prisoners' dilemma and agency theory – but there are others as well. As I see it, these new developments show beyond any doubt that it is the economists who are in the forefront when it comes to innovations in the social science use of the concept of interest.

According to a famous formulation, modern economics rests 'upon the granite of self-interest', but there are some reasons to believe that this metaphor may not be the most appropriate one (Stigler 1975: 237). For one thing, economics has developed from being mainly concerned with the self-interest of the individual, and how this self-interest can be realized, to becoming a *perspective* of the analyst, summed up in the expression of 'rational choice'. What primarily matters in modern economics is the rational choice of the actor, based on the actor's perfect knowledge of the fallout of various alternatives. Secondly, as mainstream economics has solidified around the assumption that the actor is in a position to make a rational choice, based on her economic self-interest, some critique of this view has also been voiced. Economic behaviorists and others have, for example, shown that the idea of rational self-interest provides a much less stable foundation than what the metaphor of granite suggests.

In a series of articles from the 1970s onwards Amartya Sen has discussed the tendency in modern economics to vacillate between a view of interest as a goal to be realized and a view of interest that is mainly concerned with the formal qualities of the choice of the actor (see especially Sen 1986). There exist two main conceptions of rational choice in modern economics, Sen explains: one that focuses on the internal consistency of the actor's decision, and another that is mainly concerned with the external correspondence of the actor's decision to her interest. What matters the most according to 'the internal consistency approach' is that the actor's preferences can be ranked in an orderly fashion (transitivity), that the actor has the information that is necessary for her choice, and the like (Sen 1986). 'The interest correspondence approach', in contrast, operates with an outside referent: the actor has an interest, and the main point is to realize this interest or, more precisely, to see how well the decision that is taken corresponds to the actor's interest.

According to Sen, the idea of consistency is not strong enough to constitute the foundation for a full theory of rationality; and the main reason for this is that it is an empty criterion. Irrational decisions that are consistent would, for example, be perfectly rational from this viewpoint. As to the interest correspondence approach, Sen argues that it is much too narrow in that it directly identifies interest with egoism. What is needed in today's economics, he concludes, is a broader version of the interest correspondence approach. Sen terms this broader version 'correspondence-rationality' and says that it is characterized by the fact that it goes well beyond economic self-interest and also includes other motives as well as identity.

The idea of revealed preference was introduced into economics by Paul Samuelson in a couple of articles in the 1930s and 1940s. It is important to include this notion in a discussion of the concept of interest because it signals a further step in the transformation that this concept has undergone during its use in economics. While economists started out by using interest in the nineteenth century, they later changed to utility and after that to marginal utility. Samuelson's theory of revealed preference represents an attempt to get rid of the concept of utility once and for all, and to replace it with that of preference. In his pioneer article from 1938 Samuelson states that he wants 'modern economics' to eliminate 'the last vestiges of the utility analysis' (Samuelson 1938: 62).

Samuelson's argument for switching to the notion of revealed preference is, however, not as straightforward as it might seem. On the one hand, it is clear that Samuelson wanted to replace the notion of utility with that of preference. But there is also the fact that if preferences are identical to behaviour, one can do away with the notion of preferences altogether and only speak of behaviour. Samuelson, however, clearly wanted to keep the notion of preference, but he did not provide his new concept with a philosophical or epistemological foundation – and this opened up the door for the argument that one can dispense with it totally.

Translated back into the language of interest, Samuelson's position can be described as follows. Interest is identical to behaviour – but interest is also a form of decision or rational choice. The concept of revealed preference is a form of rational choice because, in Samuelson's formulation, what is of central importance to this concept – the very foundation on which the theory of revealed preference rests – is the idea that it is possible to make an unambiguous ranking of various alternatives. Revealed preference theory, in other words, is only possible if certain logical criteria are met, of which transitivity is the central one (Samuelson 1938).

Samuelson's writings on revealed preference theory are thoroughly non-empirical in nature but, none the less, argue for a behaviourist stance; they also rule out any reference whatsoever to the meaning with which economic actors invest their actions. What this means is that Samuelson ends up with a very flat concept of interest. What currently exists is, if not exactly the whole truth, the only thing that economics should deal with.

An interesting light is cast on Samuelson's theory of revealed preference by the argument about so-called falsified preferences. According to this argument, which was introduced by Timur Kuran (1995), the preferences that an actor displays in public may under certain conditions not be those that she would choose in private. This turns out to be a rather common phenomenon, as the existence of peer pressure and conventional behaviour remind us. There is also the important fact that other actors react to these publicly displayed preferences ('public preferences') rather than to the ones that are held in private ('private preferences'), which may lead to collective phenomena with their own distinct dynamic. Samuelson's idea of behaviour being the same as revealed preferences consequently turns out to be wrong in some cases, which can be empirically specified. Samuelson's argument is further marred by its behaviourism, especially its disregard for the meaning with which the actor invests her action.

Another development that has cast some new light on the limited way in which the concept of interest has been used in mainstream economics is that of game theory. The current version of game theory was developed after World War II and then became popular in mainstream economics in the 1970s and 1980s. Game theory differs from economic analysis in a few important ways, all of which are related to the concept of interest. First and foremost, while *homo economicus* is a lone actor and reacts only to prices (and not to people), the basic unit of analysis in game theory is an actor whose actions depends on those of another actor. More precisely, the strategy that actor A will take depends on its set of pay-offs, and each value in this set is directly related to what actor B does. On the negative side, game theoretical excuses are typically carried out without reference to empirical material. The implicit assumption is that actors in real life are faced with distinct strategies and are also aware of their respective pay-offs. Whether this is a realistic assumption to make is rarely discussed in the game theoretical literature.

The way that the concept of interest figures in game theory is, in other words, as follows: the actor wants a pay-off that is as high as possible; and she is also aware that its value is directly dependent on the actions of another actor. In itself this represents an interesting advance in relation to mainstream economics since interest in game theory is strategic and no longer just parametric. There is, however, quite a bit more to game theory and interest than this, and one way to see this is to take a look at the game known as prisoners' dilemma.

The situation that this game refers to is the following. Two actors who have committed a very serious crime, and who are kept isolated from one another in jail, are faced with the choice of either making a full confession or not; and depending on their choice, they will be sentenced to different times in jail. The pay-offs (time in jail) are tailored to the two strategies (full confession or not) in such a way that if each of the actors follows her interest (as little time in jail as possible), both of them will end up being worse off than if they had chosen not to follow their self-interest (see Figure 4.1).

Prisoners' dilemma is often seen as a game that shows that there are situations in society in which individual rationality must give way to some kind of collective agreement, similar to the situation known as the tragedy of the commons. Translated into interest theory, this means that there are situations in which individual

Figure 4.1 Prisoners' dilemma

		Prisoner 2	
		Confess	Not confess
Prisoner 1	Confess	−10, −10	0, −20
	Not confess	−20, 0	−2, −2

Note: Two criminals are kept isolated from each other in jail and face the following options. They can either confess to a major crime they have committed (twenty years in jail) or the can confess to some minor crime (two years). The result of their individual choices, however, depends on what the other person does since squealing is rewarded by the Attorney General ('it is an American story' – Sen 1982: 62). This means that the best solution for each of the two prisoners is to not confess (−2/−2). Since both follow their individual interest, however, they will confess – and be worse off (−10/−10).

interests can only be realized if an agreement has been established with the other actor(s).

But there also exists another way of interpreting the prisoners' dilemma game, and this is to view it as an example of a situation in which you need to change the existing institution in order for the actors to be able to maximize their individual interests. In this particular case, the existing institution is that of the US system of justice with a District Attorney who has the authority to create incentives for criminals to tell the whole truth and implicate one another. If criminals could have it their way, the institution would no doubt be changed so that they could communicate with one another, coordinate their lies, and get out of jail as quickly as possible.

What the prisoners' dilemma game brings to our attention, from the perspective of interest theory, is consequently the importance of institutions for the realization of interests. A poorly constructed institution will prevent the actors from realizing their interests, while a well-constructed institution will facilitate it. This insight, it should also be noted, is added to the theory of *homo economicus*, since the actors are assumed to maximize regardless of whether they happen to find themselves in a modern American system of justice or in a system of a type that they would prefer. The prisoners' dilemma, in brief, adds to the theory of interest, as this has become part of modern economics, primarily the issue of institutions – but it does so without challenging the foundation of the theory of *homo economicus*.

Agency theory constitutes a third contribution that has been made by economists to the contemporary discussion of the concept of interest. This type of theory is very flexible and can be applied to a large range of topics, including non-economic ones. Agency theory has its origin in legal theory, as many other ideas about interest (e.g. Schoch 1948). The main problem in legal theory that the concept of agency has been used to address for many centuries is the following: a person (the agent) has been hired by another person (the principal) to represent the latter towards a third person.

It was not, however, legal thinkers who brought the concept of agency to prominence in the social sciences, but the economists; and this happened in the 1970s. And while the emphasis in legal thought had been on the problem of how to conceptualize a situation in which an agent is able to enter a contract with a third party that is, none the less, binding for the principal, the economists shifted the focus to another link in the agency–principal relationship. To them the key problem in agency is as follows: when a principal hires an agent to carry out something that is in her interest, what is there to ensure that this will indeed be done, given that the agent has interests of her own?

The economists have also suggested a few ways in which the interest of the agent can be made more similar to that of the principal ('alignment of interests'). One of these is to introduce special incentives for the agent, in order to make sure that she acts in the interests of the principal. Another is to monitor or directly check that the agent does not deviate from the interest of the principal.

As already mentioned, agency theory is so broad that it can be applied to a large number of topics. Economists have mostly used it to analyse the firm and especially how CEOs can be made to operate effectively in the interest of the owners, instead of giving themselves perks and in other ways prioritizing their own interest. In a famous article on this problem it is, for example, argued that CEOs must be rewarded as owners if they are to behave like owners; if they are 'paid like bureaucrats', they will 'act like bureaucrats' (Jensen and Murphy 1998: 270). Analyses have also dealt with other groups in the firm than CEOs. Workers, for example, have been conceptualized as agents, with foremen playing the role of monitors; and sales people have been seen as agents who are paid a commission, as opposed to a salary, in order to align their interests with that of their principal.

How flexible the notion of agency theory is can also be illustrated by a recent attempt to explain trust, which draws on the idea that the interests of an agent and a principal do not totally overlap. While most agency theorists focus on that part of the interest of the principal and the agent that does *not* overlap, and discuss what consequences this lack of overlap may possibly have, one may also do the opposite and single out what happens with the part that *does* overlap. This is what Russell Hardin suggests in a recent work on trust, which is centred around the notion of 'trust as encapsulated interest' (Hardin 2002). The basic idea is that you trust someone because you think that the other person has a good reason to maintain the relationship, in the sense that it is in her interest to take your interest into account. The owner of a house, for example, may have good reason to trust that the cleaning person will not steal, since the cleaning person needs a regular income. The cleaning person, in brief, 'encapsulates' the interest of the owner (no theft) into her own interest.

There is a generality to agency theory that makes it easy to transfer it to the other social sciences. It is easy enough, for example, to see how sociology and psychology can suggest other mechanisms than those of incentives and monitoring through which the interests of the principal and the agent may be aligned (e.g. through various forms of bonding, identification, and so on). Agency theory also shows that it makes sense, also in modern economics, to use the term 'interest' under certain circumstances and not replace it with more specified terms.

In a discussion such as this of what has happened to the concept of interest in modern economics, it is also necessary to include something about the critique of the assumption of self-interest. This critique goes way back to the nineteenth century, when it was articulated very strongly by sociologists, historians and rebel economists. What will be discussed here, in contrast, are some recent attempts within mainstream economics itself to challenge the assumption of self-interest. The argument of these critics is not so much that this assumption is always wrong and should be discarded, but that it is clearly wrong in *some* cases, and that these cases are frequent enough to warrant a discussion of the assumption of self-interest.

One of these critiques comes from the field of behavioural economics, which has grown into rapid prominence during recent years. Some of the main arguments against the automatic assumption of self-interest can be found in the work of behavioural economists on what they call loss aversion, mental accounting and the role of fairness in economic life (e.g. Camerer, Loewenstein and Rabin 2004). Loss aversion refers to the fact that people have been found clearly to prefer to avoid losses to acquiring less gains, when the same sum of money is involved. Mental accounting covers situations in which the same amount of money is treated differently, depending on what mental category the actor files it away in – as windfall profit, hard-earned salary and so on. Fairness, finally, enters in some economic transactions in a very clear manner. One example of this would be the situation in which some employees are being fired; and while this is seen as acceptable and just in some situations (e.g. when the firm is doing very poorly), it is seen as unfair in others (e.g. when the firm is doing fine).

Behavioural economics is often accused of accumulating anomalies rather than constructing a general theory of economics, and there is some truth to this. From the perspective of the discussion of the concept of interest, it can also be noted that behavioural economists basically interpret their results in terms of psychology and aim most of their critique at what they see as the unrealistic behavioural foundations of economics. To some extent this self-identification as psychologists rather than, say, as sociologists, is also reflected in the preference among the practioners of behavioural economics for experiments as opposed to surveys, comparative work, and the like.

Another critique from inside mainstream economics that has been directed at the concept of self-interest in modern economics is based on the notion of *identity*. The basic idea here is that a person's identity must be taken into account in certain situations when it comes to understanding the interest of an economic actor (e.g. Akerlof and Kranton 2000). According to Amartya Sen, the identity of an actor matters for the following reason: it can influence 'what the person sees his interest to be and what effects that might have on his choices' (Sen 1986: 74).

Since I will be returning to Sen's concept of identity later in this chapter, it may be useful to explain briefly what he means by this last statement. Sen notes, for example, that there may exist contemporary societies in which the interest of the family overtakes the individual interests of its members. Similarly, a person in a modern corporation may see her interest from the perspective of being a team member rather than from that of the lone, maximizing individual. And finally, people may more generally interpret their interests differently, depending on whether they view themselves as members of a certain class, a certain community, and so on. Sen's advocacy of identity, in brief, points in the direction of the social, while psychology is the main reference point for the behavioural economists. The causality in Sen's argument goes from the social context to identity; from identity to perception of interest; and from perception of interest to (rational) choice.

The Role of Interest in Political Science

The most important social science, besides economics and sociology, when it comes to making frequent use of the concept of interest, is political science. This discipline has produced one very successful concept – that of interest group – which has become part of everyday language and also spawned a large literature of empirical studies. Much more discussion and analysis have also been devoted to the concept of interest in political science than in any of the other social sciences. This last statement also includes economics, even though the concept of interest plays a much more important role in standard economics than it does in the average political science analysis.

In what follows I shall first say something about the concept of interest group, and then proceed to public choice, which uses the concept of interest in a very different way from traditional political science. I will end by giving two examples of the type of thorough and illuminating discussion of the concept of interest that one can only find in the political science literature (readers interested in the discussion of interest outside the social sciences, say, in philosophy, may for example consult Frankel Paul, Miller and Paul 1997).

If someone can be said to be the father of the interest group approach, it is surely Arthur Bentley whose ideas were discussed in Chapter 3 as part of the discussion of Gustav Ratzenhofer's work. In *The Process of Government* (1908) Bentley broke with the tradition in political science to focus on the institutional and constitutional features of government and emphasized instead the importance of groups in political life. This was clearly a major achievement for which Bentley deserves credit. Bentley, however, spoke about groups in general rather than political groups; and for this reason (and some others as well) his ideas did not immediately translate into what today is known as interest group research.

The person who revived Bentley's ideas and produced the first major work on interest groups is David Truman, and he did so in *The Governmental Process* (1951). This work also inspired an avalanche of studies on interest groups and made this type of research the main focus of US political science. Democracy, from this perspective, does not only mean voting and what the government does; citizens can also influence the political process by forming interest groups. According to the theory of pluralism, which had its heydays in the 1950s and the 1960s, interest groups and other political groups balance each other and together give voice to the citizens in a democracy (e.g. Connolly 1969; for a critique, see Balbus 1971).

Truman's work implicitly helped to popularize the standard definition of an interest group as a group or organization that attempts to influence public policy. This definition has often been criticized for making the concept of interest very flat by giving it a narrow, operational definition. Truman himself tried to avoid this by introducing the concept of 'shared attitudes' into the notion of interest. An attitude, according to Truman, does not necessarily entail an interaction, and this means that when we state that a group has an interest, we not only refer to what it expresses through its activities but also to what it would like to accomplish. Truman's full definition of interest group reads as follows: ' "interest group" refers to any group, that on the basis of one or more shared attitudes, makes certain claims upon other groups in society for the establishment, maintenance or enhancement of forms of behavior that are implied by the shared attitudes' (Truman 1951: 33).

According to a recent survey of the literature on interest groups in political science, this type of research reached its peak in the US in the 1950s and the first half of the 1960s (Baumgartner and Leech 1998). Since then it has declined and moved from the core of the discipline to its margins. However, studies of interest groups and lobbying are being produced today. There exist a huge number of contemporary studies on this topic, including high quality research of special interest groups as well as the ways in which the process of mobilization takes place. Still, when it comes to theory and ruling paradigms, interest groups are not any longer at the centre of what is happening in political science.

While interest has been used in mainstream political science primarily to create a middle-range concept (interest group) that can easily be used in empirical studies, it has also been used in a very different way in another approach to political analysis. This is in public choice analysis where interest is used as in mainstream economics, namely as the foundation for a universal type of analysis that only allows for self-interest as a driving force. Public choice has been called 'politics without romance', and this nicely captures some of its spirit. To this should also be added that while public choice is analytically strong, it is often empirically weak, again like economics (e.g. Lewin 1991).

Mancur Olson's *The Logic of Collective Action* (1965) is one of the most relevant studies in the public choice tradition when it comes to a discussion of the concept of interest. The argument in this well-known work is that even if individuals may want to form a group to defend their interests, such a group will typically *not* be formed, and the reason for this is that it is not in the individual interest of the actors to support this type of project. For each individual actor it is cheaper to let others do the work and be a free rider. Olson explicitly attacks Arthur Bentley's ideas and notes that *The Process of Government* exclusively speaks about group interests and not about individual interests. There only exists one way to create organizations that defend the interests of a large number of individual members, he also argues, and that is to separate out those who are willing to pay for the organization from those who are not. This, he argues, can be done through so-called selective incentives.

The Logic of Collective Action was perceived as a massive attack on the literature on interest groups, and thanks to Olson this type of study was discredited and pushed to the margins of the discipline. The existence of an interest does not automatically translate into the formation of an interest group; the latter has first to mobilize its members, and this is an uphill battle since individual interests and collective interests do not automatically coincide. The elegance of Olson's argument and its analytical punch assured its success.

But Olson's argument has also been criticized on several grounds. One is that Olson fails to deal with history (e.g. Hirschman 1982). According to another line of criticism, the argument about the free rider does not take identity into account. Identity can be understood in many ways, and the critics of Olson essentially take it to mean something that is qualitatively different from self-interest, not just another version of self-interest as in Sen's argument about identity. Identity, in brief, refers to what is value-rational rather than instrumentally rational, to use the terminology of Weber (e.g. Pizzorno 1978, Brubaker and Cooper 2000).

Another criticism that has been directed at Olson's argument is close to the position of behavioural economics in that it argues that people sometimes follow their interests in a rational manner and sometimes do not. As opposed to behavioural economics, however, the presence or absence of rationality in the pursuit of one's interests is seen as the result of a social process and not as an anomaly. As an example of this type of criticism, one can mention the research result that while most people do not free ride, students of economics do (Marwell and Ames 1981). A theory about free riders, in other words, seems more congenial to those who have already been taught that human beings behave in a rational way.

While Mancur Olson's study must be seen as an important achievement in modern political science, it does not exhaust what modern political scientists have to say on interest. I am in particular thinking of the discussion of the concept of interest that one can find in the political science literature during the last few decades. While economists largely take the meaning of interest for granted, and while sociologists only discuss it occasionally, political scientists have had a much more extensive discussion of its different uses, if and how it can be operationalized, how it can be improved and so on. To give a sense of this type of literature I will present two examples, one article by William Connolly and another by Philippe Schmitter.

In *Theories of Political Discourse* William Connolly devotes a long and important section to a discussion of the use of interest in contemporary political science and political philosophy (Connolly [1974] 1993). There exist a few major approaches to this problem, according to Connolly, and each has some merits as well as drawbacks. One of these approaches is to view interest as identical to policy preferences; and this constitutes the most popular way to deal with interest in political science (1: 'Interests as Policy Preference'). This way of proceeding, Connolly notes, lends itself to empirical analysis in a very natural manner. On the negative side, it fails to capture the fact that certain policy measures are taken for moral reasons while others are taken for reasons of self-interest.

There also exist groups in society that do not get to formulate their policy preferences for one reason or another; and these appear – wrongly, according to Connolly – as not having any interests.

Another common way in political science to conceptualize interests is from a utilitarian perspective (2: 'Utilitarian Interests'). One version of this approach can be found in the work of Brian Barry, who argues that something is in the interest of some person 'if it increases his opportunities to get what he wants – whatever that may be' (Connolly [1974] 1993: 53; cf. Barry 1969: 163). By defining interests in this manner you can, for example, easily handle the situation that an actor may be doing something for moral reasons, while another does it out of self-interest. Using this perspective, it also becomes possible to handle the situations in which an actor mistakes her interest and acts in a way that leads nowhere. One clear drawback to Barry's approach, on the other hand, is that it does not allow for the fact that action may be taken for other reasons than interest, such as friendship and trust. Barry, as Connolly notes, takes the common position that friendship and trust can be adequately conceptualized in terms of self-interest, and this is definitely wrong.

Should interests rather be defined as needs then? Connolly argues that there exist some advantages to this way of proceeding; and it makes it easier, for example, to draw a clear line between, on the one hand, egoistic needs and, on the other hand, a person's needs for friendship, love and the like (3: 'Interests as Need Fulfilment'). But there are also drawbacks to the concept of interests as needs, according to Connolly. While it may be relatively easy to determine what the basic needs of human beings are, this type of exercise becomes very difficult once you come to the rest of people's needs. The need approach is also problematic, Connolly says, in that it precludes the idea that the actor has the capacity to reason about the alternatives she faces.

This reflective capacity is very important to Connolly, who argues that it has to be part of the way that interest is conceptualized. Only if this is the case does it become possible to grasp what the true interests of an actor are (4: 'Real Interests'). The way to find out which these interests are is by proceeding as follows. Let us imagine a situation in which the actor knows *in advance* the outcome of the various strategies that are open to her; she is then in a position to make a true choice and realize her real interests.

While this way of conceptualizing real interests is problematic, to say the least, Connolly should, none the less, be credited with having brought counterfactuals into the discussion of interests. In trying to locate the real interests of an actor, he also presents a more convincing argument than many Marxists do, when they speak about 'the false consciousness' of the working class, its failure to realize its 'objective interests' and the like.

As my second example of a work by a political scientist that contains an important discussion of the concept of interest, I have chosen an unpublished paper by Philippe Schmitter on the theory of interest politics from the early 1980s (Schmitter 1981). Schmitter's scholarship is mainly concerned with so-called organized interests, a type of organization that is typically conceptualized in a way that differs from that of interest groups. Organized interests are fewer in number than interest groups and also more long-lasting; key actors typically include labour and capital. Furthermore, while organized interests are often associated with a view of society in terms of corporatism and *Realpolitik*, interest groups tend to be associated with a pluralist approach to politics and a liberal view of reality (e.g. Berger 1981).

Schmitter's paper on the theory of interest politics contains, just like Connolly's article, a discussion of existing approaches to the concept of interest in political science as well as an attempt to present a new approach. Current theories of interest are, for example, criticized on the ground that they are either operationalized to the point of being theoretically empty or theorized in a substantive manner but difficult to use in empirical studies. The idea that one can define interest in terms of some other phenomena, say, needs or wants, is also vain, according to Schmitter; and one reason for this is that interests are fundamentally processual in nature.

Schmitter's own proposal for what an improved concept of interest may look like is thoroughly processual in nature. The key idea is that human beings have many different needs, and that these must be narrowed down through successive stages. Schmitter suggests that the analyst should start out from the needs and proceed from these to interests; then go from interests to concerns; from concerns to action; and from action to associations. He describes this step-wise reduction from needs to actions and associations as a *funnel* (see Figure 4.2). Schmitter adds that one must distinguish between the analytical order of these steps and the order in which they take place in history. While needs precede interests in the funnel, in history interests typically shape needs.

Figure 4.2 Philippe Schmitter's interest funnel

N E E D S

I N T E R E S T S

C O N C E R N S

A C T I O N S

ASSOCIATIONS

INTERMEDIATION
OF ORGANIZATIONAL
PRIVILEGED INTERESTS

Note: According to Philippe Schmitter, one way to approach the analysis of organized interests is to conceptualize the notion of interest as a kind of funnel. From this perspective, the analysis of interest is fundamentally processual in nature. The analyst starts from a multitude of needs, and then proceeds from these, through successively more concrete steps, to actions, which can be mediated via interest organizations.
Source: Schmitter (1981).

Schmitter's theory about interests as part of a larger process that is shaped like a funnel has many positive qualities to it. It is, for example, social in a complex way. While needs are individual and non-social, according to Schmitter, they must be translated into interests, and these are thoroughly social:

> Interests are social in several senses of that term. They normally involve interaction with others – whether cooperative or antagonistic – and, hence, the theory of causality upon which they are constructed must take into account the behavior of others. It must be assumed that others are also reflecting on their needs and defining their interests. From this generalized 'interest game' of past experiences and anticipated reactions, the theorist/evaluator must identify (within the bounds of limited knowledge, time, etc.) the appropriate *Interessenlage*, to use the expression of Max Weber. (Schmitter 1981: 23)

Finally, Schmitter also highlights the reflective dimension of interest through his argument that interests must be seen as 'reflection on needs' (*ibid.*: 20). What Schmitter calls 'concerns' are similarly defined as 'actors reflecting on their interests' (*ibid.*: 47). Actions inspired by custom, strong emotions or moral obligations, in contrast, lack the element of reflection. Interests and concerns, in brief, are to a certain extent driven by reflection.

Turning the Discussion of Interest in a New Direction

As I see it, the works of Connolly and Schmitter reflect the current state of the art when it comes to the concept of interest in today's social science literature. Both are also in agreement that this concept needs to be improved, especially in the way that it is defined or conceptualized. Connolly and Schmitter, however, only get so far in their discussions. Connolly's suggestion that an actor has to know the end result of her strategies in order to be in a position to know her real interests is clearly unrealistic. For a number of reasons, it is impossible for people to know what will happen when they act, and Connolly's suggestion must therefore be rejected.

Schmitter's processual approach to interest avoids the charge of being unrealistic, but has some other drawbacks. One of these is that Schmitter operates with a much too long chain of causality – from needs to interests, to concerns, to actions, and so on – and this reduces the power of his argument. There is also the fact that if you decide to follow Schmitter's approach in an empirical study, you are likely to end up by only looking at the last few parts of the funnel (concerns, action, associations); and the reason for this is that the earlier parts are quite far away from what happens in reality (needs, interests). Finally, a concept such as need is old-fashioned and awkward to work with.

How then is one to proceed? My own view is that it is important to develop a concept of interest or a way of looking at interest that decisively breaks with old-fashioned notions such as wants, needs and the like; and it is also important to apply a way of thinking to interest that is more in line with the twenty-first century. A new way of looking at interest should ideally be able to keep what is fruitful and positive about the current notion of interest – but discard the rest.

The traditional way to determine the meaning of a concept is to define it in terms of one or several other concepts, and proceed from there. This way of approaching a concept, however, goes sharply counter to the current state of knowledge about what constitutes the meaning of a word or a concept. The idea of a one-to-one correspondence of some sort has long since been discarded, and it is also understood that the meaning of any word is very difficult to nail down. Meaning has its own distinct phenomenology which cannot be ignored; and this is especially true for the concept of interest, since it has been part of so many contexts over the centuries.

One way to avoid the old-fashioned way of defining a concept is suggested by Wittgenstein in *Philosophical Investigations*. This is to look at the uses of a term, and in this fashion get closer to its meaning. This approach is common in the social sciences today, and it is definitely preferable to the one-to-one type of definition as well as the idea that one can somehow give an exact definition of a concept. On the negative side, however, is the fact that there have been so many different uses of the concept of interest that one may not get very far by trying to determine which these are. A further complication is that it is much more problematic than it might seem to determine what the uses of a concept are, and what these mean.

Philosophical Investigations, however, also suggests a different way to proceed, even if it only does this implicitly. This is to work with analogies, which in the case of Wittgenstein meant to get at meaning in language by comparing it to a special case of social activity, namely a game. Wittgenstein motivates bringing in the notion of a language game by referring to the fact that '*the speaking of language is [like a game] part of an activity, or of a form of life*' (Wittgenstein [1953] 1958: 11; emphasis added). Following this way of proceeding, I will similarly argue that one way to get a better grip on the meaning of interest may be to introduce an analogy to it, which is also that 'part of an activity, or of a form of life'.

The analogy – the special activity or form of life – that I have in mind for the case of interest is that of *following a sign-post*. The situation that the concept of interest attempts to capture includes actors, a sign-post and the act of following the direction of the sign-post. The term 'sign-post' (*Wegweiser*), incidentally, is a term that Wittgenstein also uses in *Philosophical Investigations*, although in a different sense from how I use it here. While I use the analogy of following a sign-post as part of an attempt to get at the meaning of interest in the sense of a distinct activity, Wittgenstein introduces it to make the point that the rules that make up a language game are open ended and only cover some cases, as opposed to all cases. But just as a signpost may seem to give sure directions of where to go, but in reality only indicates a general direction, rules for how to use language may seem to cover all possible cases, but in reality only some of these (*ibid.*: 39–40).

The analogy of a language game is used by Wittgenstein, as just mentioned, in an attempt to point out that the meaning of something does not come from the fact that a word somehow represents or mirrors a particular piece of reality (from which it would get its meaning). Meaning is rather part of an *activity* or something that includes more than words ('the *speaking* of language is part of an activity, or of a form of life'). Similarly, the analogy of actors following a sign-post is not introduced in order to somehow capture the essence of the *word* 'interest', but to indicate that the meaning of interest is to be found in *a certain type of activity*.

Two points in this last statement need to be explicated. First it is crucial to stress – and this is something that Wittgenstein does not do – that actors' decisions to follow a certain direction are not only 'activities', as this word is commonly understood, but that they always mean that the actors *physically* take this direction, body and all. When actors decide to pursue their 'interests', they do so with themselves and their bodies at stake; and it is precisely this that gives their efforts its force as well as its existential dimension. 'Following one's interest' means, in brief, that words and actions go together, and that these two also have to be analysed together (Øygarden 2000). Interest without the body becomes a purely mental activity, for which the word 'interesting' – as in reading an interesting book – is more appropriate.

Second, in the analogy I suggest the actors are assumed to possess a distinct and special level of consciousness, as indicated by the fact that they are following a sign. As I will soon elaborate if interest means that people do something with their bodies, and not only with their minds, they also have to have a special mindset for the activity to qualify as an 'interest'.

The three key components that make up the situational analogy that is suggested here are the actors, the signpost and the activity of following the direction of the signpost. Actors, however, can also be motivated by other forces, such as habit, tradition and affect, in which case the influence of their interests on their behaviour is low and does not account for its direction. In this case, you do something because you are used to doing it or because it is the tradition to do so, and so on. This was presumably often the case in early societies where tradition was strong and rarely challenged. The more aware that the actors are of having their own distinct interests, however, the more they will also attempt to realize these in a deliberate manner. They will try to figure out what their interests are and what to do with them – in brief, they will try to figure out in which direction they need to go in order to realize them.

A signpost is therefore only followed by actors who know their interests and want to realize them. Actors must orient their behaviour to the signpost and this also presupposes that they have the capacity to decide whether to follow it or not. Most will take the general direction, but some will not. There is also the fact that there are about as many signposts as there are interests: religious, economic, political, sexual and so on. Actors may travel in many directions; and a totally private interest will typically be harder to realize than one that is publicly acknowledged.

The signpost has a physicality or resistance to it that the purely mental deliberations of the individual actor lack. This is to be understood in the sense that a signpost signifies what is outside the individual actor and her immediate control, even if it is still the creation of other actors. Everything social that is outside the control of the individual actor will have this quality of objectivity and also show resistance to change from the side of the individual actor. What adds to the resistance – and objectivity – of the signpost as a social fact is the legitimacy that comes with just having been around for a long time.

The individual actor attempts to follow and realize her interests, but she may mistake the direction in which she needs to travel, in order to do this. Not only do you have to decide on what signpost to look for; you also have to map out the exact road to take, and each individual has to do this herself. While Wittgenstein, to repeat, uses the analogy of the signpost for a different purpose than I do, what he has to say about the vagueness of the sign-post is, none the less, relevant. According to *Philosophical Investigations*:

> A rule stands there like a signpost. – Does the sign-post leave no doubt open about the way I have to go? Does it shew which direction I am to take when I have passed it; whether along the road or the footpath or cross-country? ... And if there were, not a single sign-post, but a chain of adjacent ones of chalk marks on the ground – is there only *one* way of interpreting them? – So I can say, the signpost does after all leave no room for doubt. Or rather: it sometimes leaves

> room for doubt and sometimes not. And now this is no longer a philosophical proposition, but an empirical one. (*ibid.*: 39–40)

This is again a point at which the social intervenes in the attempt to realize an interest. Depending on the society, group and so on, of which the actors are part, they will find it natural to take one way rather than another. And to find this way, they also have to consult other actors along the way – another point at which the social becomes important.

To find their way the actors clearly must have a certain mental disposition, just as they need to have a certain mental disposition to decide what their interests are and that they want to realize these. This mental state is described in a suggestive way by Weber in his discussion of *Interessenlage* as a form of 'distinct awareness and lack of feeling bound' ('*Bewusstheit und inneren Ungebundenheit*'; Weber [1922] 1972: 15). Another way to describe this awareness would be to say that it consists of a certain mental alertness and a readiness (and capacity) to think and act in a deliberate manner. And again, there is an obvious social dimension to this awareness and freedom: you can only develop it under certain conditions, and it only exists in certain groups, societies, and so on.

Just as there are many signposts that point in many directions, there also exist many different ways to proceed once you have decided where to go. Given the fact that attention in the debate about interest is nearly always restricted to one single type of interest – to self-interest, which is associated with acting in an instrumental way – it is important to note that there also exists a radically different type of consciousness and lack of being bound. This is the road taken by actors whose goals are seen as ends in themselves (values) and as being so important that efforts to reach them are made regardless of the possibility of success. Your goal may have been set by God or some other deity. So, just as there are social actions that are instrumentally rational and value-rational (Weber), interests can be seen as instrumentally rational as well as value-rational. By proceeding in this manner, the concept of interest is expanded and becomes closer to the meaning it once had ('ideal and material interests').

Finally, the end result of many actors trying to realize their interests raises a number of questions that cannot be answered simply by looking at the individual actor and her actions. Patterns are created and new interests may emerge as the result of the collective processes involved when many actors travel in the same direction. Weber's work is instructive on this point as well, especially his sociology of religion. Many actors may start their religious journey with the same goal – to reach salvation – but end up with very different results, both for the society in which they live and for themselves. What will happen depends, among other things, on what the switchmen have been up to. According to *The Protestant Ethic*, the spiritual efforts of Catholic lay people typically end up by reinforcing the traditional dimension of the economy, just as the equivalent efforts of ascetic Protestants typically end up by reinforcing its dynamic dimension.

When many individual interests come together, it is clear that unintended consequences will start to accelerate. Above I used Weber's sociology of religion to indicate one way in which to proceed when this happens; you focus on the way that religious and economic activities are linked. Another would be to go to the work of Thomas Schelling and draw on his many suggestions for how micro-motives may turn into different types of macro-behaviour (Schelling 1978). More generally, this is a point in the discussion of interests where you have to bring in the notion of social mechanisms (e.g. Hedström and Swedberg 1998).

Three Examples

Before ending this small book I will attempt to show the continuing relevance of the concept of interest by presenting some examples where it can be used to address important social science problems. The concept of interest, as I see it, still has much to offer, and its potential has by no means been exhausted. One of the examples I have chosen has to do with institutions and how these should be conceptualized; another deals with situations in which ideas can turn into powerful social forces; and the third is about the problem of objectivity and how this can be ensured. I will also try to show how these examples illustrate the relevance of seeing interest as a distinct 'activity or form of life' (Wittgenstein).

The definition of institution that I want to criticize and try to improve on is the standard version that can be found in political science, sociology and to some extent also in economics. It basically says that an institution consists of a set of rules; that actors follow these rules; and that there are formal as well as informal rules. What I consider problematic with this type of definition is precisely that it does not mention interests but speaks exclusively of rules. If interests are removed from the picture, pretty much anything that is governed by rules has to be termed an institution, including a dance, a way of greeting people or blowing your nose. This way of proceeding, as I see it, trivializes the idea of institutions and argues implicitly that people do what they do primarily because of the existence of rules and a desire to follow rules.

Once interests are introduced into the picture, however, institutions become fewer in number and also more relevant to people's key concerns. Institutions, I suggest, can provisionally be viewed as rules for how to realize interests. The main interests in any society include political and economic interests; there are also reproductive interests (realized through the institution of the family) and religious and similar interests (realized through religious and similar organizations). Institutions are typically regarded as so important to the functioning of society that they are regulated in law. To be truly effective they also need to be legitimate, and this essentially comes about through supportive norms and beliefs. Institutions, in brief, can be understood as *legitimate rules or models for how to realize interests*.

The analogy of actors following a signpost allows us to add a few points to this general picture. For one thing, institutions narrow down the actions that are undertaken by the actors in their attempts to reach their goals. Institutions also make it very costly to take alternative roads, by treating these as breaches of law and/or convention. The force that individual actors bring to their efforts – the fact that they invest their energies and put their bodies on line in the pursuit of some specific interest – translates into the great social weight that is characteristic of institutions. The fact that many actors take the route for granted and as the only right way to proceed (legitimation) adds considerably to this weight or force.

One may also argue that institutions come further down the road, so to speak, when actors try to realize their interests. You first have to decide what your interests are and then how to go about realizing them. Some institutions are fundamentally traditional, and these are hard to change, precisely because traditional actors have less of a sense of what their interests are. They lack awareness as well as a sense of not being bound. Modern institutions, in contrast, are easier to change, precisely because modern actors are much more aware of their interests and have a sense of being Promethean or unbound. Traditional institutions make actors walk in a circle; modern institutions are made for actors with distinct goals.

Another case where I feel that an interest approach has much to offer, and where this has not been fully realized, has to do with ideas and their potential power. Ideas can be of two kinds: those that describe some aspect of the world, and those that do this and are also somehow linked to the interests of actors. If an idea becomes linked to an interest, that is, if it somehow becomes connected to the interests of individuals, it will also be invested with the force of these interests. A classical example of this is Weber's *The Protestant Ethic* in which the focus is precisely on how ideas become fused with interests, first religious interests and then also economic interests, with revolutionary consequences for the social and economic structure.

James Coleman has applied his micro-to-macro model to the argument in *The Protestant Ethic*, and this allows me to make my point about ideas and interests (Coleman 1990: 8). Coleman begins by showing how Weber's analysis goes from the collective level (Protestant attitudes) down to the level of the individual (Step 1); how the impact of these ideas on the individual then spreads from her religious behaviour to her economic behaviour (Step 2); and, finally, how the interaction of many individuals eventually result in the creation of a new attitude on the collective level (Step 3; see Figure 4.3).

One can, however, also cast this type of analysis in terms of interests. If we do this, it becomes possible to see how ideas on the collective level, under certain circumstances, can connect to the religious interests of the individual (Step 1); how these ideas eventually also get linked to economic interests (Step 2); and how this, on the collective level of attitudes, leads to a new attitude to economic interests or the creation of the spirit of rational capitalism (Step 3).

The analogy of following a signpost may help to tease out a few more features. The force that ideas may acquire, when they are fused with interests, derives from the fact that the actors invest them with their bodies and full efforts. This is especially so in case of *The Protestant Ethic*, where we begin with a value-rational type of action (inspired by religion), which then blends with, and becomes amplified by, the force of an instrumentally rational type of action (inspired by a desire for wealth). Both the kind of religion that Weber discusses (ascetic Protestantism) and the kind of capitalism

Figure 4.3 How ideas and interests may come together, according to *The Protestant Ethic*

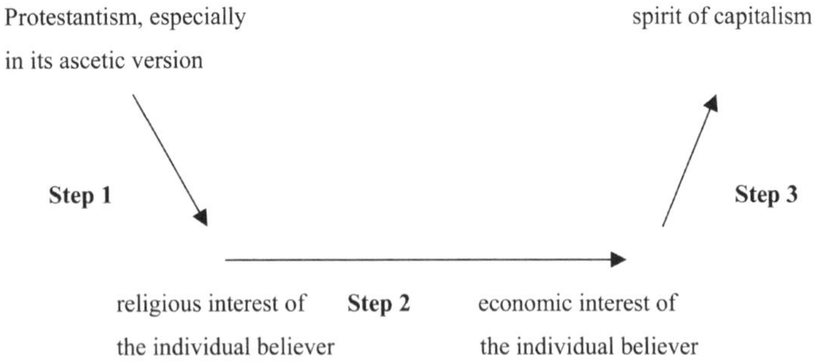

Note: In *The Protestant Ethic* Weber shows how ideas, when joined to interests, may become extremely strong social forces. The case that Weber analysed illustrates how certain religious ideas helped to break the hold of religion over the economy and usher in modern rational capitalism. The figure should be read as follows: the individual believer is first exposed to the new religious doctrine of Protestantism (especially in its ascetic version) and relates these ideas to her religious interest (Step 1). She will eventually also apply them to her economic interest (Step 2). The economic actions of many individuals, all driven by their combined religious–economic interests, eventually create a new economic ethic, namely the spirit of capitalism (Step 3).

that he has in mind (rational capitalism) have a similar mentality: a high degree of alertness or awareness, in combination with a sense of not being bound. As with institutions, Weber's analysis is about a situation in which interests are given a direction.

My third and last example is about objectivity in the social sciences. The classical position on this issue is often associated with Weber's position that the social scientist should make an effort to suppress her values in her lectures and social science writings, especially those that are related to politics. This is known as value neutrality (*Wertneutralität*). To this Weber added that it was clear, none the less, that the scientist's choice of topic is related to the values in the society in which she lives; and this he termed value relevance (*Wertbeziehung*). Later sociologists have sometimes added that the social scientist should also make a conscious effort to see how her ideas have been formed by her background and experiences (reflexivity). In this manner, it is argued, she will be in a better position to locate a few more sources of possible biases.

There also exist some attempts to approach objectivity from a less individualistic perspective, and as examples of this one can mention Karl Mannheim's argument about free-floating intellectuals as well as Robert K. Merton's notion of the ethos of science (Mannheim [1936] 1960: 136–46; Merton [1938] 1973). Both of these attempts, however, are similar to the ideas of value-neutrality and reflexivity in one respect; and this is in their negative attitude to interests, which are seen as something that must be eliminated as much as possible for there to be objectivity. The free-floating intellectuals, according to Mannheim, are not as anchored in economic class interests as the majority of people are, and it is precisely this that makes it possible for them to be objective. Merton similarly tells us that a key component in the ethos of science is 'the norm of disinterestedness'. More generally, Merton sees scientists as being driven by a desire for status and peer approval in their pursuit of science, rather than by a desire for money and property. The world of science is characterized among other things by 'communism' or the notion that all ideas are freely available.

While the standard stance in the social sciences seems to be that interests prevent objectivity, and that they therefore should be suppressed, one may also argue that interests can further objectivity. One example of this would be the adversarial system of law, which can be found in common law countries. The idea here is that the best way to ensure that justice is done is to have both parties present their arguments in court as forcefully as possible, and that the judge or the jury will then make a judgment based on the facts that have been produced in this manner. This way of proceeding contrasts with the so-called inquisitorial system that is common in continental law countries, in which it is the judge who carries out the investigation. In the latter type of system, cross-examination and plea bargaining do not exist.

Another example of making a positive use of interests, in order to ensure objectivity, can be found in the idea that it is necessary to have many scholarly journals, scientific societies and the like. This way of proceeding is sometimes cast in terms of using social institutions as a means of creating scientific objectivity, as opposed to relying exclusively on individual character as, for example Weber does (e.g. Popper 1962: 218). It may, however, also be seen in terms of using individual interest to further the general interest along the lines of Adam Smith in *The Wealth of Nations*. From this perspective, objectivity is what pays off for the individual scientist as well as being a by-product of her actions. The strategy, from this perspective, is to create a situation in which there is much 'competition', little 'collusion' and no 'monopoly' in the world of science. Objectivity, in other words, is furthered by interests balancing each other.

Objectivity, from an interest perspective, may then be seen as an agreed-upon road to take, given that scientists have certain goals that they want to reach (fame, wealth, deference and so on). As long as following the road of objectivity can lead to these goals, objectivity is to some extent guaranteed. Once this is no longer the case, however, objectivity will be endangered.

Concluding Remarks

The concept of interest has been used for a very long time and can on one level be described as a way of talking and thinking about the way that people have come to pursue fundamental goals and values. While the term 'interest' was originally a legal and not a popular term, it has over the centuries been used both by specialists and other people. This is still the case, although I have spent little effort in this study to document the popular use of the term 'interest', in politics or elsewhere (but see for example the comment on the use of 'special interests' in Nunberg 2003).

For the social science concept of interest the many different uses that this term has gone through over the centuries should represent a strength. Economists, sociologists and other social scientists have found the concept of interest useful in different ways, and among the individuals who have used it are to be found some of the best minds in the Western tradition. My sense is that much is still to be learned from this tradition and that it can serve as a source of inspiration for new and important uses of the concept of interest.

Different strategies have evolved in the social sciences for how to use the concept of interest. First and foremost, economists have used it to lay the foundation for their science. In order for this to work, the concept of interest has had to be narrowed down to economic interest, and other influences than interests have had to be excluded. An enormous weight has in this way been put on the concept of interest and much critique has been directed at this type of analysis.

During the last few decades a discontent with the exclusive concern in economics with economic matters has been growing, as exemplified by the emergence of public choice and the work of scholars such as Gary Becker and George Akerlof. Many important advances have been made by using an expanded concept of economic interest, as exemplified by agency theory and the theory of collective action. I say 'expanded' since non-economic interests are analysed along the lines of economic interests.

The second main strategy when it comes to using the concept of interest in the social sciences has been to turn it into a middle-range concept; and as examples of this one can mention the notion of interest groups and Weber's concept of action orientation determined by self-interest (*Interessenlage*). By proceeding in this way, considerably less weight is put on the concept of interest. There is clearly also a better fit between middle-range concepts of this type and various empirical practices in society, than between *homo economicus* and equivalent practices. On the other hand, it would seem that the latter approach has been better at fuelling the creativity of social scientists.

Despite this last statement about economists being better at innovating with the help of the concept of interest, I have been unable to find much discussion of this concept in the economists' camp. The contrast on this point with political science is striking. Political scientists have engaged in important discussions of how to operationalize interest, how to conceptualize 'objective' interests, what distinguishes moral concerns from economic interests, and the like.

My own suggestion for how to breathe some new life into the discussion of interest is to break sharply with the old attempt to somehow pin down the meaning of this concept through some new and clever definition. I argue that definitions of the old type do not fit a concept such as interest, which over the centuries has been used by social scientists, writers and many other groups of people. Wittgenstein's argument that meaning resides in a distinct *activity*, in contrast, allows us to better capture what interest is all about. This is especially the case if we take the position that interest is something that people are doing, not only in their minds but also in activities that involve their whole being. When things matter, you put your body behind your words; and pursuing an interest is a case of this type of acting.

Wittgenstein's suggestion to use a specific analogy to turn the discussion of meaning in a new direction – to understand language not simply as words strung together but as an activity similar to that of a game – may also be a useful tactic when it comes to interest. The analogy that I have proposed for interest is that of actors following a sign-post telling them where to go. While this analogy may seem lacklustre and uninteresting to some readers, I would insist, none the less, that it directs our attention to something that is essential about the notion of interest. This is that it involves a certain type of activities in which only people with a special kind of consciousness can engage, and which they also do with body and soul. Interests have to do with the direction that individuals choose to follow in life. To the question 'What are people's interests?' I would answer: locate where people are physically and determine whether they act with the type of consciousness that Weber describes as Promethean or not being bound. The research task, in short, is to capture a special activity in which people engage – not to hunt down the meaning of a word (intcrest).

The social element intervenes at a number of obvious points in this type of activity. One of these is why some individuals have this special type of consciousness and decide to act on it. Another is that there exists a kind of Promethean awareness in certain societies, but not in others. In realizing their interests people also look to institutions for a first answer and therefore orient their behaviour to these. And they typically have to orient their actions to other actors in order to realize their interests.

What is common to all of these social dimensions to interest-driven behaviour is their core, which is also existential in nature. In *Critique of Dialectical Reason* Sartre argues that interest represents a false kind of consciousness. The actor, he says, has simply exteriorized her desires and, in doing so, subordinated these to an outside and seemingly objective force (Sartre 1976: 197–219). This, however, is not what I have in mind when I say that there is an existential dimension to interest. I argue instead that in realizing any interest you have to put your body on the line in one way or another; it is not enough to think or play with words. And it is precisely this quality of waging your existence that accounts for the great realism that is characteristic of interest analysis, especially since you are not only involving your own body and mind but also those of others. The result is insight into the human struggle and existence of a type that has fascinated thinkers over the centuries.

5

Addendum: Interest as a Policy Tool – A Case Study

In the earlier chapters I have dealt with interest as a tool of analysis that can be of assistance in making it easier to explain social reality. But interest can also be used as a policy tool, that is, as a guide (or sign-post) to consciously change social reality in some desired direction. In this addendum I will discuss this type of situation in some detail, and there are several reasons for doing so. First of all, it is important to make clear that interest has a social engineering side to it that deserves to be part of the discussion. Secondly, there is the question of whether reforms based on the concept of interest have been successful. There is also the fact that the discussion of interest as an analytical concept should be related to the attempts to change reality with the help of this concept.

From what has just been said it is clear that a series of important as well as interesting questions attach to interest as a policy concept. To answer these through a discussion of the type that has been carried out in the earlier chapters is, however, not possible due to the lack of literature on the topic. It has therefore seemed best to approach this type of question by discussing a concrete case study, and go from there.

The foremost example of a case where interest has been used to change social reality is probably the US Constitution with its attempts to balance various interests against each other and thereby create a political system that makes it hard to abuse power. This, however, constitutes a case much too complex to be discussed in a short book such as this, so I have chosen another, more modest example, which plays, none the less, an important role in contemporary society. This is conflict-of-interest legislation or the type of legislation that is made to ensure that people are not allowed to hold certain positions if they have some private interest that may interfere with the proper performance of their tasks.

While the term 'conflict of interest' is a familiar one, it only recently leapt to universal attention in the US when it came to play a major role in the media coverage of the corporate scandals involving such companies as Enron and WorldCom. Much of what had gone wrong with these and many other corporations, it was soon discovered, had precisely to do with the destructive role of conflicts of interest.

In the next few pages I will discuss the two most important cases of these corporate scandals which began in 2001 and are still going on. These are the accounting industry and the brokerage industry. I will first say a few words about the notion of conflict of interest and its origin; then present the situation in the US accounting industry and brokerage industry which led to a violation of conflict-of-interest legislation; and finally conclude by saying something about the way that the idea of interest can be used as a policy tool.

The Concept of Conflict of Interest in Legal Thought and in Public Discourse during the Corporate Scandals in the United States (2001–)

The current edition of *Black's Law Dictionary*, which is the most authoritative dictionary in North American law, defines 'conflict of interest' as follows:

> 1. A real or seeming incompatibility between one's private and one's public or fiduciary duties. 2. A real or seeming incompatibility between the interests of two of a lawyer's clients, such that the lawyer is disqualified from representing both clients if the dual representation adversely affects either client or if the clients do not consent. (Garner 1999: 295)

An important theme that informs conflict-of-interest legislation is that misconduct will not take place in every case where there is a conflict of interest, but in enough cases for there to be reason to try to interfere *before* anything goes wrong. Conflict-of-interest legislation is, in other words, prophylactic in nature; and what matters, to cite a Supreme Court decision from 1961, is not so much what 'actually happened' as what 'might have happened' (*US* v. *Mississippi Valley Generating Company*; cf. Stark 2000: 4).

The legal concept of conflict of interest has its own history, which is largely unwritten. It is clear, none the less, that this notion has its origin in early legal thought; and there are those who argue that the idea of conflict of interest goes all the way back to the Middle Ages. The term that was used during this time, however, was 'ambidexterity', and it 'literally referred to lawyers, "ambidexters", who took money with each hand from different parties to a dispute' (Rose 1999: [2]). In 1789, during the first Congress in the US, an Act was passed according to which the holder of the newly instituted office of Secretary of the Treasury could not invest in government securities. Much American conflict-of-interest legislation dates to the second half of the nineteenth century, and to the attempts to create an efficient government after the Civil War.

The legal term 'conflict of interests' seems, however, to be considerably younger than the idea of such a conflict. When it first emerged is difficult to say and may vary depending on the area of application. By the 1950s conflict of interest was, however, a generally accepted legal term in the US. Two standard works on the subject were published around this time.

The great novelty with the use of the term 'conflict of interest' during the last few years in the US is that it has become part of public discourse in describing several economic phenomena, to which it had earlier not been applied. More generally, in the discussions surrounding the current corporate scandals in the US, the concept of conflict of interest has been central from the very beginning. It has not only become part of the vocabulary of the media but can also be found in the speeches and writings of many public figures, including George W. Bush, George Soros and Joseph Stiglitz. This means that the awareness of conflicts of interest is currently very high, which also affects the possibility of using it as a policy concept.

The two situations where one can find the term 'conflict of interest' used the most frequently, in the popular media as well as in the work of official commentators, is in connection with the following two industries: accounting (especially in situations where the same firm does both accounting and consulting) and brokerage firms (especially in situations where these sell stocks on behalf of some clients and also advise other clients about which stocks to buy). In the Sarbanes-Oxley Act of 2002, which was created in response to the current corporate scandals, these two industries are also discussed as important examples of industries in which conflicts of interest are common and need to be regulated.

The Background to the Conflicts of Interest in the Corporate Scandals

What drove the conflicts of interest in the accounting and brokerage industries was first of all the boom on the stock exchange in the 1990s and the greed that this created. The rapid rise in the price of shares set off the kind of self-interested behaviour that led to conflicts of interest. A number of important institutional changes also took place during this decade which operated in the same direction. In 1999 the Glass-Steagall Act (1933) was formally repealed and also industries other than banking were deregulated. Ordinary bank business could, for example, now be combined with investment banking, and so could ordinary brokerage business. As the stock market rose, initial public offerings became increasingly common – and also an excellent source of income for brokerage firms and banks.

During the 1990s the stock exchange quickly shot upwards; Dow Jones quadrupled and the Nasdaq increased by more than 800%. In January 2000 the Dow Jones Industrial reached the record high of 11722.98, and in March 2000 Nasdaq Composite reached a peak of 5048.62. At this time many CEOs received part of their pay in options, and for the first time in US history it was now possible for CEOs to become extremely wealthy without being entrepreneurs, creating new corporations or the like. This was the period of 'irrational exuberance', to cite a phrase by Alan Greenspan which has become something of a symbol for the boom in the 1990s.

But in 2000 the stock market started to decline, and a series of spectacular corporate meltdowns and bankruptcies soon took place that were much discussed in the media. The first of these was Enron, which went bankrupt in December 2001, and the largest was WorldCom, which went bankrupt half a year later. It soon also became clear that a huge number of corporations had inflated their profits, with the help of various accounting devices ('aggressive accounting'). In particular WorldCom's announcement in mid 2002 that it had inflated profits by $3.8 billion caused fury in the media and among investors.

All in all, what mainly drove the conflicts of interest in

accounting and business analysis was the boom on the stock exchange in the 1990s, in combination with deregulation and an atmosphere of *laissez-faire*. All of this added to the temptation for individuals and firms to make money quickly and set caution aside. There was an outcry of anger when a number of these wrongdoings were found out, and this public outcry led to the passage of the Sarbanes-Oxley Act in 2002 which forbade and criminalized some of this behaviour.

Conflicts of Interest in the Accounting Industry and the Brokerage Industry

The problem in the accounting industry was centred around the fact that the US accounting industry had increasingly begun to do consulting for the very same firms whose books they were auditing. This development, which had started after World War II, endangered the soundness of accounting since it was difficult to be objective about a firm in which one also had a direct economic interest. The danger of this situation was well understood by various observers and actors in the US, and had often been discussed. All attempts, however, to deal with this situation through legislation had been blocked by the accounting industry, which wanted to keep its right to self-regulation.

During the 1990s this conflict between accounting and consulting was sharpened by the boom and several accounting firms became involved in dubious or illegal activities. The most famous of these involved Arthur Andersen, the accounting firm of Enron and one of the largest accounting firms in the US. What made Arthur Andersen set caution aside was precisely that Enron was seen as a great source of income, most of which came through consulting. Enron was well aware of this situation and used it to its advantage. Through various accounting tricks, illegal acts by the Enron leadership were repeatedly covered up by the staff of Andersen. When these were discovered the US Justice Department took Andersen to court and had it convicted, which took place in June 2002. Since an accounting firm that has been convicted for a felony is not allowed to do business, Andersen was effectively forced into bankruptcy. At the time when this happened, Andersen had branches in 84 countries, $9.3 billion in revenue, 26,000 employees in the US and 84,000 worldwide.

The conflict of interest in the US brokerage industry was of a different nature from the one in the accounting industry. What was at issue here was, in brief, whether a firm can both sell shares on behalf of certain clients and at the same time advise other clients about what shares to buy and sell. During the boom of the 1990s it had become increasingly common for brokerage firms to do precisely this, and it was well understood on Wall Street that the analysts at the brokerage houses were deeply influenced in their suggestions for what to buy and sell by other business activities that were going on at their firms. Brokerage firms would, for example, argue that the shares of some firm represented an excellent investment opportunity, even if this was not true, simply because they hoped to do business with the firm some time in the future or had a long-standing relationship with it.

In 2002 the Attorney General of the state of New York, Eliot Spitzer, uncovered a large number of e-mails from business analysts on Wall Street that showed that they were well aware of the fact that their analyses were often deeply biased and that the reason for this was that they let themselves be influenced by the interests of their employers. If a brokerage firm, for example, knew that one of its clients was in trouble, they would tell their analysts to hide this fact and recommend people to buy the stocks.

Spitzer threatened the major brokerage firms on Wall Street with conviction in court, which would have closed them down for good. In response to this threat, they allowed themselves to be collectively fined a sum of $1.5 billion. Part of this amount was to be used, Spitzer specified, to support independent analyst firms and investor education. Spitzer also made several suggestions for how the brokerage firms should be changed, in order to guarantee objective analysis in the future.

Attempts to Solve the Conflicts of Interest

A large number of proposals for how to solve the conflicts of interest in the accounting and business industries were made in response to the corporate scandals in the US. The most important piece of legislation that has been used to deal with these issues is the Sarbanes-Oxley Act of 2002. There is also Eliot Spitzer's decision to take the main brokerage firms to task for their illegal behaviour in the autumn of 2002. Of the many other initiatives a special mention should be made of Paul Volcker's effort to solve the conflicts of interest at Arthur Andersen in the spring of 2002 since this represents an important attempt to develop a model for the whole accounting industry.

There is a distinct complexity to the many proposals for how to solve the many conflicts of interests that were part of the scandals in the US, and it may therefore be useful to introduce a simple typology. The proposals can be sorted into four categories, depending on their stance on two issues. There is first the question of whether one should use law or self-regulation to solve conflicts of interest. There is also the question of whether one should assign different economic activities to different organizations or allow these activities to coexist in the same organization but separated by a so-called 'Chinese Wall' (a self-enforced separation of activities). The most common outcome of the scandals has been a strengthening of the 'Chinese Wall' through self-regulation, which also represents the traditional way for the securities industry and the accounting industry to handle conflicts of interest (see Table 5.1 for the different alternatives).

Table 5.1 Different ways of handling conflicts of interest in the accounting and brokerage industries

	'Chinese Wall'	**Different functions in different firms**
Law	1	2
Self-regulation	3	4

Note: Conflicts of interest in the accounting and brokerage industries can either be handled through legislation or self-regulation; and the two activities can either be allowed to coexist in the same firm ('Chinese Wall') or be assigned to different firms.

According to the Sarbanes-Oxley Act of 2002, potential conflicts of interest are to be handled through 'Chinese Walls' (1). A few suggestions for radically separating the two activities were made in Congress early in 2002 as well as by Eliot Spitzer (2). Before the Sarbanes-Oxley Act most conflicts of interest in accounting and brokerage firms were handled through self-regulation, typically in the form of a Chinese Wall (3). Self-regulation in combination with assigning different functions to different firms was suggested by Volcker in the spring of 2002 for the whole accounting industry, using Andersen as his model (4).

Attempts to solve the conflicts of interest began as soon as Enron collapsed and it became clear that investors – including several major pension funds – had lost billions of dollars. Some politicians advocated legislation to put an end quickly to conflicts of interest in accounting for good; and in early 2002 several proposals were made in Congress to forbid accounting and consulting from being done by one and the same organization, to let the state take over auditing through the creation of a Federal Bureau of Audits, and the like.

For various reasons, proposals for legislation of this type had little chance of resulting in something tangible in the US Congress. From the very beginning of the crisis the accounting industry also launched a heavy lobbying effort to preserve the self-regulation of the industry and minimize the impact that any new legal measures might have; and the lobbying arm of the accounting industry is well known for its efficiency. The Bush administration was sensitive to the public outcry over the scandals but reluctant at this particular point to address the issue of conflicts of interest.

Under the impact of new scandals that kept happening one after the other during the spring and summer of 2002, the Bush administration, however, decided to take measures. The signing into law on 30 July of the Sarbenes-Oxley Act was the major result of this resolve. According to Bush, this law represented 'the most far-reaching reforms of American business practices since the time of Franklin Delano Roosevelt' (Bush 2002).

From the Sarbanes-Oxley Act and various speeches by Bush it is clear that the US government's perception of the corporate scandals was primarily in terms of individual responsibility. According to the new law, CEOs must vouch for the annual financial statements of their firms. The penalty for white-collar crimes, committed by those in charge of a corporation, was also dramatically increased to a maximum of 20 years. From around mid 2002 it has also become increasingly common in the US media to see managers being led away in handcuffs – another indication that the Bush administration wanted to let the public know that it had become tough with those who were engaged in 'corporate corruption'. This tendency to focus on the individual actor continued through the autumn of 2002, and in his State of the Union address in 2003 Bush again lashed out at 'corporate criminals' (Bush 2003).

But even if the Sarbanes-Oxley Act has been shaped to a large extent by the need for what Bush and his administration termed 'a new ethic of personal responsibility in the business community', it also contains several paragraphs expressly devoted to more structural issues such as conflicts of interest in accounting as well as in business analysis. According to the new law, in particular, there has to be a stronger 'Chinese Wall' between consulting and accounting as well as between brokerage and business analysis. A new institution has also been created whose task is to oversee the accounting activities of major corporations, the so-called Public Company Accounting Oversight Board. The general purpose of this board is 'to protect the interests of investors and further the public interest in the preparation of informative, accurate and independent audits' (US Congress 2002: 6). The board has the power either to create standards of accounting and auditing or to adopt existing ones from self-regulating agencies.

Finally, an interesting effort to find a solution to conflicts of interest in accounting was made by Paul Volcker, the former head of the Federal Reserve, in the spring of 2002. Volcker, who was hired by Andersen in 2002 to clear up its problems, essentially wanted to split off consulting from accounting in Andersen, and thereby end the possibility for conflicts of interest once and for all. He also had high hopes that this way of proceeding would become a model for the rest of the industry. Volcker's plan can be called self-regulation by example. Since Andersen, however, refused to plead guilty, and since the Justice Department refused to withdraw its indictment, Volcker's plan was more or less doomed to fail. Volcker would later say that he had received no support for his efforts from corporate America and that the whole thing, in hindsight, 'was a dream, like Don Quixote' (Labaton 2002).

Concluding Discussion

It is clear that conflict-of-interest legislation does not cover all situations in which interests collide and clash, but only a small sample of these. More precisely, conflict-of-interest legislation is primarily aimed at handling situations in which there is a potential conflict between some private interest and the general interest that an actor has been set to guard.

As the examples that have just been discussed show, there are situations in which these attempts at legislation have not been very successful. In both the accounting industry and the brokerage industry, for example, there were structural forces at work which made it tempting for actors to cross the line and satisfy some private interest at the expense of the general interest. Complexity was added to the situation by the fact that in these cases there were three interests involved: the general interest of the public (especially but not exclusively investors), the private interest of the individual actor (analysts, accountants, etc.), and the private interest of the firm (legal personality). The pressure of the firm to make a profit was typically transmitted to some employee, who had to make a choice about what to do.

The reactions to the corporate scandals in the US show some of the options that were open to those who wanted to bolster the conflict-of-interest legislation in order to block wrongdoing and steer private interests away from the general interest. To what extent the Sarbanes-Oxley Act is effective in doing this will be shown in the future, especially when there is a new boom of the type that occurred in the 1990s.

When it comes to the terminology suggested in this book, it is clear that conflict-of-interest legislation can be understood in terms of the earlier discussion of interest, namely as an analogy to a situation in which you have actors following a sign-post. As any sign-post, conflict-of-interest legislation cannot specify what the actor is to do. It does, however, steer the actor away from certain activities; it tells the actor what situations to avoid and where not to go.

The desire to construct a social situation in terms of conflicts of interest, it may finally be noted, also grows out of the insight that self-interest often needs to be tempered with a certain dosage of moral values, if society is not to be harmed. As mentioned earlier, Tocqueville noted that the Americans did this primarily with the help of religion. According to Tocqueville, in this way the Americans succeeded in steering self-interest in a useful and non-destructive direction. The result he termed ‘self-interest properly understood’.

As a form of social engineering the idea of conflicts of interest is useful in that it allows some activity to be pursued, while the destructive uses of the same activity are successfully neutralized; and this is accomplished by balancing two interests against one another. In *The Federalist* (1787–88) James Madison argued for a separation of powers in the American Constitution, and he referred to arrangements of this type as ‘inventions of prudence’ (Hamilton, Jay and Madison 2001: 269). The idea of a conflict of interests may similarly be termed an ‘invention of prudence’, and as such it has an important role to play in modern society. A different but more memorable way to express the very same idea can be found in James Buchanan's famous reply to a journalist who asked him what major insight had earned him his Nobel Prize. Buchanan said: 'Don't put the fox in charge of the chicken coop.'

References

Akerlof, George and Rachel Kranton. 2000. 'Economics of Identity', *Quarterly Journal of Economics* 15: 715–53.

Arrow, Kenneth. 1987. 'Rationality of Self and Others in an Economic System', pp. 201–16 in Robin Hogarth and Melvin Reder (eds), *Rational Choice*. Chicago: University of Chicago Press.

Balbus, Isaac. 1971. 'The Concept of Interest in Pluralist and Marxian Analysis', *Politics and Society* 1: 151–77.

Barry, Brian. 1969. 'The Public Interest', pp. 159–77 in William Connolly (ed.), *The Bias of Pluralism*. New York: Atherton Press.

Baumgartner, Frank and Beth Leech. 1998. *Basic Interests: The Importance of Groups in Politics and in Political Science*. Princeton, NJ: Princeton University Press.

Bentham, Jeremy. 1843. 'The Springs of Action', pp. 195–219 in Vol. 1 of *The Works of Jeremy Bentham*. Edinburgh: William Tait.

Bentham, Jeremy. 1948. *The Principles of Morals and Legislation*. New York: Hafner Press.

Bentley, Arthur. 1908. *The Process of Government: A Study of Social Pressures*. Chicago: University of Chicago Press.

Berger, Suzanne (ed.). 1981. *Organized Interests in Western Europe: Pluralism, Corporatism, and the Transformation of Politics*. Cambridge, MA: Cambridge University Press.

Borges, Jorge Luis. 1964. 'The Analytical Language of John Wilkins', pp. 101–5 in *Other Inquisitions 1937–1952*. Austin: University of Texas Press.

Boudon, Raymond and François Bourricaud. 1989. 'Utilitarianism', pp. 419–23 in *A Critical Dictionary of Sociology*. London: Routledge.

Bourdieu, Pierre. [1971] 1987. 'Legitimation and Structured Interests in Weber's Sociology of Religion', pp. 119–36 in Sam Whimster and Scott Lash (eds), *Max Weber, Rationality and Modernity*. London: Allen & Unwin.

Bourdieu, Pierre. [1981] 1990. 'The Interest of the Sociologist', pp. 87–93 in *In Other Words: Essays Towards a Reflexive Sociology*. Cambridge: Polity Press.

Bourdieu, Pierre. [1988] 1998. 'Is a Disinterested Act Possible?' pp. 75–91 in *Practical Reason*. Cambridge: Polity Press.

Bourdieu, Pierre. 1993. *Sociology in Question*. London: SAGE.

Bourdieu, Pierre. 2000. *Das religiöse Feld. Texte zur Ökonomie des Heilgeschehens*. Konstanz: UVK.

Bourdieu, Pierre. 2005. 'Principles of an Economic Anthropology', pp. 75–89 in Neil Smelser and Richard Swedberg (eds), *The Handbook of Economic Sociology*. 2nd rev. edn. New York and Princeton: Russell Sage Foundation and Princeton University Press.

Bourdieu, Pierre and Loïc Wacquant. 1992. *An Invitation to Reflexive Sociology*. Chicago, IL: University of Chicago Press.

Brubaker, Rogers and Frederick Cooper. 2000. 'Beyond "Identity"', *Theory and Society* 29: 1–47.

Bush, George W. 2002. 'President Announces Tough New Enforcement Initiatives for Reform'. 9 July. http://www.whitehouse.gov/news/releases/2002/07/20020709-4.html.

Bush, George W. 2003. 'President's State of the Union Message for Congress and the Nation', *New York Times* 29 January: A12.

Camerer, Colin, George Loewenstein and Matthew Rabin (eds). 2004. *Advances in Behavioral Economics*. Princeton, NJ: Princeton University Press.

Coleman, James. 1984. 'Introducing Social Structure into Economic Analysis', *American Economic Review* 74, 2: 84–8.

Coleman, James. 1986. *Individual Interests and Collective Action: Selected Essays*. Cambridge: Cambridge University Press.

Coleman, James. 1990. *Foundations of Social Theory*. Cambridge, MA: Belknap Press.

Connolly, William (ed.). 1969. *The Bias of Pluralism*. New York: Atherton Press.

Connolly, William. [1974] 1993. 'Interests in Politics', pp. 45–84 in *The Terms of Political Discourse*. 3rd edn. Princeton, NJ: Princeton University Press.

Demeulenaere, Pierre. 1996. *Homo Oeconomicus. Enquête sur la Constitution d'un Paradigme*. Paris: Presses Universitaires de France.

Demeulenaere, Pierre. 2001. 'Interest, Sociological Analysis of', pp. 7715–18 in Vol. 11 of Neil Smelser and Paul Baltes (eds), *International Encyclopaedia of the Social & Behavioral Sciences*. Amsterdam: Elsevier.

DiMaggio, Paul. 1988. 'Interest and Agency in Institutional Theory', pp. 3–21 in Lynn Zucker (ed.), *Institutional Patterns and Organizations*. Cambridge, MA: Ballinger.

Edgeworth, Francis Y. [1881] 2003. 'Mathematical Psychics', pp. 1–150 in *Mathematical Psychics and Further Papers on Political Economy*. Oxford: Oxford University Press.

Emirbayer, Mustafa. 1997. 'Manifesto for a Relational Sociology', *American Journal of Sociology* 103: 281–317.

Foucault, Michel. 2001. *Fearless Speech*. Los Angeles, CA: Semiotext(e).

Frankel Paul, Ellen, Fred Miller Jr. and Jeffrey Paul (eds). 1997. *Self-Interest*. Cambridge: Cambridge University Press.

Frisby, David. 2004. E-mails to Richard Swedberg on the relationship between Georg Simmel and Gustav Ratzenhofer.

Garner, Bryan. 1999. *Black's Law Dictionary*. 2nd edn. St Paul, MN: West Publishing Company.

Gunn, J.A.W. 1969. *Politics and the Public Interest in the Seventeenth Century*. London: Routledge.

Habermas, Jürgen. 1971. *Knowledge and Human Interests*. Boston, MA: Beacon Press.

Hamilton, Alexander, John Jay and James Madison. 2001. *The Federalist*. Indianapolis, IN: Liberty Press.

Hardin, Russsell. 2002. *Trust and Trustworthiness*. New York: Russell Sage Foundation.

Heckathorn, Douglas. 1990. 'Collective Sanctions and Compliance Norms', *American Sociological Review* 55: 366–84.

Hedström, Peter and Richard Swedberg (eds). 1998. *Social Mechanisms: An Analytical Approach to Social Theory*. Cambridge: Cambridge University Press.

Heilbron, Johan. 1998. 'French Moralists and the Anthropology of the Modern Era: On the Genesis of the Notions of "Interest" and "Commercial Society"', pp. 77–106 in Johan Heilbron *et al.* (eds), *The Rise of the Social Sciences and the Formation of Modernity*. Amsterdam: Kluwer.

Helvétius, Claude-Adrien. [1758] 2000. *De l'Esprit; or, Essays on the Mind*. Bristol: Thoemmes Press.

Hirschman, Albert O. 1977. *The Passions and the Interests: Political Arguments for Capitalism before its Triumph*. Princeton, NJ: Princeton University Press.

Hirschman, Albert O. 1982. *Shifting Involvements: Private Interest and Public Action*. Princeton, NJ: Princeton University Press.

Hirschman, Albert O. 1986. 'The Concept of Interest: From Euphemism to Tautology', pp. 35–55 in *Rival Views of Market Society*. New York: Viking.

Holmes, Stephen. 1990. 'The Secret History of Self-Interest', pp. 267–86 in Jane Mansbridge (ed.), *Beyond Self-Interest*. Chicago, IL: University of Chicago Press.

House, Floyd. 1926. 'The Concept of "Social Forces" in American Sociology. Section V. The "Interest" Concept', *American Journal of Sociology* 31: 507–12.

Huber, Beat. 1958. *Der Begriff des Interesses in den Sozialwissenschaften*. Wintherhur: Verlag P.G. Keller.

Hume, David. 1966. *Enquiries Concerning the Human Understanding and Concerning the Principles of Morals*. Oxford: Clarendon Press.

Hume, David. [1739–40] 1978. *A Treatise of Human Nature*. Oxford: Clarendon Press.

Hume, David. 1985. *Essays: Moral, Political and Literary*. Indianapolis, IN: Liberty Press.

Jensen, Michael and Kevin Murphy. 1998. 'CEO Incentives: It's Not How Much You Pay, But How', pp. 270–98 in Michael Jensen, *Foundations of Organizational Strategy*. Cambridge, MA: Harvard University Press.

Knight, Frank H. [1921] 1971. *Risk, Uncertainty and Profit*. Chicago, IL: University of Chicago Press.

Knight, Frank H. 1932. 'Interest', pp. 131–44 in Vol. 7 of E.R.A. Seligman and Alvin Johnson (eds), *Encyclopaedia of the Social Sciences*. New York: Macmillan.

Kuran, Timur. 1995. *Private Truths, Public Lies: The Social Consequences of Preference Falsification*. Cambridge, MA: Harvard University Press.

La Rochefoucauld. [1665] 2001. *Maximes*. Trans. S. Warner and S. Douard. South Bend, IN: St Augustine's Press.

Labaton, Stephen. 2002. 'Can A Bloodied S.E.C. Dust Itself Off Now and Get Moving?', *New York Times* December 16: C2.

Lenin, Vladimir. [1902] 1969. *What is to Be Done? Burning Questions of Our Movement*. New York: International Publishers.

Lepenies, Wolf. 1988. *Between Literature and Science: The Rise of Sociology*. Cambridge: Cambridge University Press.

Lewin, Leif. 1991. *Self-Interest and Public Interest in Western Politics*. Oxford: Oxford University Press.

Lukács, Georg. [1923] 1971. *History and Class Consciousness*. Cambridge, MA: MIT Press.

MacIver, Robert M. 1932. 'Interests', pp. 144–8 in Vol. 7 of E.R.A. Seligman and Alvin Johnson (eds), *Encyclopaedia of the Social Sciences*. New York: Macmillan.

Mannheim, Karl. [1936] 1960. *Ideology and Utopia: An Introduction to the Sociology of Knowledge*. London: Routledge & Kegan Paul.

Marwell, Gerald and Ruth Ames. 1981. 'Economists Free Ride, Does Anyone Else? Experiments on the Provision of Public Goods IV', *Journal of Public Economics* 15: 295–310.

Marx, Karl. [1842] 1975. 'Debates on the Law on Thefts of Wood', pp. 224–63 in Vol. 1 of Karl Marx and Frederick Engels, *Collected Works*. New York: International Publishers.

Marx, Karl. [1847] 1955. *The Poverty of Philosophy*. Moscow: Progress Publishers.

Marx, Karl. [1847] 1977. 'Wage Labour and Capital', pp. 197–228 in Vol. 9 of Karl Marx and Frederick Engels, *Collected Works*. New York: International Publishers.

Marx, Karl. [1852] 1978. 'The Eighteenth Brumaire of Louis Bonaparte', pp. 99–197 in Vol. 11 of of Karl Marx and Frederick Engels, *Collected Works*. New York: International Publishers.

Marx, Karl. [1859] 1970. *A Contribution to the Critique of Political Economy*. New York: International Publishers.

Marx, Karl. [1867] 1906. *Capital: A Critique of Political Economy*. New York: The Modern Library.

Marx, Karl. 1964. *Economic and Philosophical Manuscripts of 1844*. New York: International Publishers.

Marx, Karl and Fredrick Engels. [1848] 1976. 'The Communist Manifesto', pp. 477–519 in Vol. 6 of Karl Marx and Frederick Engels, *Collected Works*. New York: International Publishers.

Mauss, Marcel. [1925] 1990. *The Gift: The Form and Reason for Exchange in Archaic Societies*. New York: W.W. Norton.

Menger, Carl. [1871] 1976. *Principles of Economics*. New York: New York University Press.

Merton, Robert K. [1938] 1973. 'Science and the Social Order', pp. 254–78 in *The Sociology of Science*. Chicago, IL: University of Chicago Press.

Merton, Robert K. 1968. *Social Theory and Social Structure*. New, enlarged edn. New York: The Free Press.

Merton, Robert K. 1984. 'Socially Expected Duration: A Case Study of Concept Formation in Sociology', pp. 264–83 in Walter W. Powell and Richard Robbins (eds), *Conflict and Consensus*. New York: The Free Press.

Meyer, John. 2000. 'Globalization: Sources and Effects on National States and Societies', *International Sociology* 15: 233–48.

Meyer, John and Brian Rowan. 1977. 'Institutionalized Organizations: Formal Structure as Myth and Ceremony', *American Journal of Sociology* 83: 340–63.

Meyer, John and Ronald Jepperson. 2000. 'The "Actors" of Modern Society: The Cultural Construction of Social Agency', *Sociological Theory* 18: 100–20.

Mill, John Stuart. 1961. *Essential Works of John Stuart Mill*. Ed. Max Lerner. New York: Bantam Books.

Mill, John Stuart. 1988. 'The Admission of Women to the Electoral Franchise 20 May, 1867', pp. 151–62 in Vol. 28 of John Stuart Mill, *Collected Works*. London: Routledge.

Mill, John Stuart. 1992. *Essays on Some Unsettled Questions of Political Economy*. Bristol: Thoemmes Press.

Molière, Jean Baptise (Poquelin). [1673] 1907. 'The Hypocondriac', pp. 179–309 in Vol. 8 of *The Plays of Molière*. Edinburgh: John Scott.

Montesquieu, Charles de Secondat. [1748] 1989. *The Spirit of the Laws*. Cambridge: Cambridge University Press.

Myers, Milton. 1983. *The Soul of Modern Economic Man: Ideas of Self-Interest, Thomas Hobbes to Adam Smith*. Chicago, IL: University of Chicago Press.

Neuendorff, Hartmut. 1973. *Der Begriff des Interesses. Eine Studie zu den Gesellschaftstheorien von Hobbes, Smith und Marx*. Frankfurt am Main: Suhrkamp.

Nietzsche, Friedrich. 1986. *Human, All Too Human*. Trans. R.J. Hollingdale. Cambridge: Cambridge University Press.

Nunberg, Geoffrey. 2003. 'The Lost Vocabulary of Disinterested Politics', *New York Times* 14 September: wk3.

OED. 1989. 'Interest-Interestingness', pp. 1099–1100 in Vol. 7 of *Oxford English Dictionary*. Oxford: Clarendon Press.

Olson, Mancur. 1965. *The Logic of Collective Action: Public Goods and the Theory of Groups*. Cambridge, MA: Harvard University Press.

Orth, E.W. *et al*. 1982. 'Interesse', pp. 305–65 in Vol. 3 in Otto Brunner *et al*. (eds), *Geschichtliche Grundbegriffe*. Stuttgart: Klett-Cotta.

Øygarden, Geir Angell. 2000. *Den Brukne Neses Estetik. En Bok om Boksing*. Oslo: Solum Forlag.

Pareto, Vilfredo. [1916] 1968. *Traité de sociologie générale*. Vol. XII of *Oeuvres Complètes*. Geneva: Droz.

Park, Robert and Ernest Burgess. 1921. *Introduction to the Science of Sociology*. Chicago, IL: University of Chicago Press.

Parsons, Talcott. [1937] 1968. *The Structure of Social Action*. New York: McGraw-Hill.

Persky, Joseph. 1995. 'The Ethology of Homo Economicus', *Journal of Economic Perspectives* 9, 2: 221–31.

Pizzorno, Alessandro. 1978. 'Political Exchange and Collective Identity in Industrial Conflict', pp. 277–98 in Colin Crouch and Alessandro Pizzorno (eds), *The Resurgence of Class Conflict in Western Europe Since 1968*. New York: Holmes & Meier Publishers.

Ratzenhofer, Gustav. 1898. *Die Sociologische Erkenntnis. Positive Philosophie des socialen Lebens*. Leipzig: Brockhaus.

Rogers, Kelly (ed.). 1997. *Self-Interest: An Anthology of Philosophical Perspectives*. New York: Routledge.

Rose, Jonathan. 1999. 'The Ambidexterous Lawyer: Conflict of Interest and the Medieval Legal Profession'. Draft. College of Law, Arizona State University.

Ross, E.A. 1905. *Foundations of Sociology*. New York: Macmillan.

Samuelson, Paul. 1938. 'A Note on the Pure Theory of Consumer's Behaviour', *Economica* 5: 61–71.

Sartre, Jean-Paul. 1976. *Critique of Dialectical Reason*. London: Verso.

Schelling, Thomas. 1978. *Micromotives and Macrobehavior*. New York: W.W. Norton.

Schmitter, Philippe C. 1981. 'Needs, Interests, Concerns, Actions, Associations and Modes of Intermediation: Toward a Theory of Interest Politics in Contemporary Society', Wissenschaftszentrum, Berlin. Unpublished paper.

Schoch, Magdalena (ed.). 1948. *The Jurisprudence of Interests*. Cambridge, MA: Harvard University Press.

Sen, Amartya. [1973] 1984. 'Behaviour and the Concept of Preference', pp. 54–73 in *Choice, Welfare and Measurement*. Cambridge, MA: MIT Press.

Sen, Amartya. 1982. *Choice, Welfare and Measurement*. Cambridge, MA: MIT Press.

Sen, Amartya. 1986. 'Rationality, Interest, and Identity', pp. 343–53 in Alejandro Foxley *et al.* (eds), *Development, Democracy and the Art of Trespassing*. Notre Dame, IN: University of Notre Dame Press.

Sen, Amartya. 1997. 'Foreword', pp. ix–xix in Albert O. Hirschman, *The Passions and the Interests*. 20th anniversary edn. Princeton: Princeton University Press.

Simmel, Georg. [1908] 1971. 'The Problem of Sociology', pp. 23–35 in Georg Simmel, *On Individuality and Social Forms*. Chicago, IL: University of Chicago Press.

Simmel, Georg. [1911] 1997. 'The Sociology of Sociability', pp. 120–30 in David Frisby and Mike Featherstone (eds), *Simmel on Culture*. London: SAGE.

Small, Albion. 1905. *General Sociology*. Chicago, IL: University of Chicago Press.

Smith, Adam. 1976. *An Inquiry into the Nature and Causes of the Wealth of Nations*. 2 vols. Oxford: Oxford University Press.

Sorokin, Pitirim. 1928. *Contemporary Sociological Theories*. New York: Harper & Brothers.

Stark, Andrew. 2000. *Conflicts of Interest in American Public Life*. Cambridge, MA: Harvard University Press.

Stigler, George. 1975. 'Smith's Travels on the Ship of State', pp. 237–46 in Andrew Skinner and Thomas Wilson (eds), *Essays on Adam Smith*. Oxford: Clarendon Press.

Swedberg, Richard. 2005. 'Conflicts of Interest in the U.S. Brokerage Industry', pp. 187–203 in Karin Knorr Cetina and Alex Preda (eds), *The Sociology of Financial Markets*. New York: Oxford University Press.

Tocqueville, Alexis de. [1835–40] 2000. *Democracy in America*. Trans. and ed. Harvey Mansfield and Delba Winthrop. Chicago: University of Chicago Press.

Tribe, Keith. 1999. 'Adam Smith: Critical Theorist?', *Journal of Economic Literature* 37, 2: 609–32.

Truman, David. 1951. *The Governmental Process: Political Interests and Public Opinion*. New York: Alfred A. Knopf.

US Congress. 2002. Sarbanes-Oxley Act of 2002. H.R. 3763. See www.findlaw.com.

Weber, Max. [1898] 1990. *Grundriss zu den Vorlesungen über Allgemeine ('theoretische') Nationalökonomie*. Tübingen: J.C.B. Mohr.

Weber, Max. [1920] 1946. 'The Social Psychology of the World Religions', pp. 267–301 in Hans Gerth and C. Wright Mills (eds), *From Max Weber*. New York: Oxford University Press.

Weber, Max. [1922] 1972. *Wirtschaft und Gesellschaft. Grundriss der verstehenden Soziologie*. Studienausgabe. Tübingen: J.C.B. Mohr.

Weber, Max. [1922] 1978. *Economy and Society: An Outline of Interpretive Sociology*. Trans. Ephraim Fischoff *et al.* 2 vols. Berkeley, CA: University of California Press.

Weber, Max. 1991. *Wirtschaftsgeschichte*. Berlin: Duncker und Humblot.

Weber, Max. 1994. *Political Writings*. Cambridge: Cambridge University Press.

Weber, Max. 1999. *Max Weber im Kontext. Literatur im Kontext auf CD-ROM 7*. Berlin: Karsten Worm InfoSoftWare.

Whimster, Sam. 2002. 'Notes and Queries', *Max Weber Studies* 3, 1: 74–98.

Wittgenstein, Ludwig. [1953] 1958. *Philosophical Investigations*. 3rd edn. New York: Macmillan.

Index